strangers assume

my girlfriend

is my nurse

also by shane burcaw

Memoir
Laughing at My Nightmare

Picture Book
*Not So Different: What You Really Want to Ask
About Having a Disability*

strangers assume

my girlfriend

is my nurse

shane burcaw

Roaring Brook Press

New York

Published by Roaring Brook Press
Roaring Brook Press is a division of Holtzbrinck Publishing Holdings
Limited Partnership
175 Fifth Avenue, New York, NY 10010
fiercereads.com

Library of Congress Control Number: 2018944885

ISBN: 978-1-62672-770-0

Our books may be purchased in bulk for promotional, educational, or business
use. Please contact your local bookseller or the Macmillan Corporate and
Premium Sales Department at (800) 221-7945 ext. 5442 or by email at
MacmillanSpecialMarkets@macmillan.com.

First edition, 2019
Printed in the United States of America

10 9 8 7 6 5 4 3 2 1

*To Squirms, for wiping my poopy butt
and still wanting to cuddle after*

Contents

Introduction

Look, I get it. Normally, I don't read introductions either, but this one is important, and I'm not just saying that because I wrote it. (Yes I am.)

There are some things you should know about me that will make your reading of this book more enjoyable.

First of all, I have a disease. The disease, which I was born with, is called spinal muscular atrophy. It causes my muscles to waste away as I get older, so I was never able to walk or even crawl. I've used a fancy schmancy electric wheelchair since the age of two, and as of writing this at the age of twenty-five, I'm starting to lose more important muscle function, like my abilities to breathe and swallow and speak.

Fun, right?

There's a whole lot more about my life and the intricacies of my disease in my first book, *Laughing at My Nightmare*. (Wow, what a dick, plugging another book he wrote on page one!) You really should read it, but I'll also give you some fast facts here that will illuminate my life history for you. I suppose a better writer would find a clever way to reveal this necessary information seamlessly within the actual essays, so that the book could truly stand alone without need for the reading of other texts, but I am not a better writer. I am merely a young man with some funny stories to tell and an annoying penchant for sarcasm. Perhaps with age I'll develop some writing chops, in addition to the lovely muscle deterioration that's in store for me.

My editor is going to love this introduction. First I try to peddle another book to you, and then I tell you I'm a shitty writer. Brilliant.

Let's see, what do you need to know?

I need help with almost every physical activity, from getting out of bed to showering to picking my nose. I've always relied on my friends and family to help me with these things, and they have always been there to help. They are phenomenal human beings. When I began writing this book, I lived with three of them: my parents—Jon and Sue—and my younger brother, Andrew. By the time I finished the manuscript, I was living a thousand miles away from them with my girlfriend, Hannah. More on that later.

Throughout a good chunk of my life, I've been trying to convince people that I'm "normal." My physique has been twisted and bent by my disease, like a plastic action figure melting in a fireplace, so from an early age, people have treated me like I'm a rolling tragedy. Strangers speak slowly to me. They assume I have no friends, no social capacity, no brain, really. People are often inspired by the fact that I'm shopping in the grocery store, as if just being outside of my house is a commendable activity worthy of praise.

In my childhood and teen years, this bothered me to no end, but it felt like an unfixable problem, so I started using jokes to avoid the issue. Humor became my coping mechanism, my solution. By cracking a joke, I could at least ease the awkward tension in most social situations, allowing kids and adults alike to see that I wasn't some precious creature that needed to be handled cautiously.

In this way, I made a great group of friends who learned to see past my wheelchair.

I played sports. I had crushes and, later on, love and intimacy. (Don't worry, there's more on that later, too.) I got in trouble. I got hurt. I went to college.

Mom, Dad, Hannah, me, Andrew, and his girlfriend, Laura, getting WILD on New Year's Eve.

In college, something unexpected happened. On a whim, I started a blog called *Laughing at My Nightmare*, and it took off into internet glory. Almost overnight (at least that's what it felt like), hundreds of thousands of people around the world wanted to read about my life and the ridiculous shit I've been through. In a way, all I was doing on my blog was what I had been doing my whole life: telling jokes to help the world understand me. People connected with my message of using humor to overcome hardship, and as enthusiasm for my story continued to grow, my cousin Sarah and I decided to start a nonprofit organization to take that message to the next level. That nonprofit, also called Laughing at My Nightmare, grew exponentially and became my full-time job after college. Today, we have a year-round speaking schedule, teaching audiences across the country the scientifically proven benefits of positivity and humor. I love it, and what's even cooler is that our organization also provides medical and adaptive equipment to individuals living with muscular dystrophy. We've donated over $80,000 in vital equipment since we began that program! Sarah and I are supported in this venture by an outstanding group of board members and employees who help us make our wild dreams a reality every day. The five years since starting that blog have been nothing short of surreal.

What else?

I have two cats, Oreo and Roxy, whom I mentioned in the

opening of my last memoir. They are both still alive, unfortunately.

As always, I hope for nothing more than to make you laugh.

Chapter 1

Eighth-Grade Pee Fiasco

The human body is disgusting.

For most, it's easy to hide our natural nastiness—secretly scraping the brown gunk out of our ears in the privacy of the shower, irrigating our nasal cavities with the sink on full blast to mask the gagging, discreetly allowing a six-second methane death bomb to squeak its way out of our sphincts while we sing Shania Twain and clip our toenails (except, in my case, for the little gray one that curled up and died a few years ago).

To be organic is to decompose, so while we may be able to mostly hide these embarrassing moments, you can know with certainty that absolutely everyone is experiencing the same things. Go ahead and imagine your mom farting in the shower now. (And you thought I had matured a little since the last book . . . guess not!)

When you have a disease like mine, your ability to hide the nastier side of being human is greatly compromised. For instance, I can't hold a tissue to my nose to blow it, so if it starts running, or if I've got a meaty cliff-hanger dangling on the outer rim for all to see, I'm stuck until I ask someone to help me, which means allowing another person into that vulnerable realm of my being.

Growing up, a majority of my care was handled by my parents. They were the ones dressing me, showering me, bathrooming me, and generally making sure I didn't smell like garbage on a daily basis. Even though there were moments in childhood when I resented needing their help (e.g., when I had to go home at 11 p.m. from my first Big-Kid Sleepover because I had accidentally pooped in my pants), for the most part, I was comfortable with their care. We had a routine, and the daily repetition felt normal.

Elementary school brought with it the shocking realization that I was expected to allow people other than my parents to help me with these private aspects of my care.

Before starting first grade, I went in to meet my new teachers. Their classrooms were colorful and bright. The teachers were friendly. They used words like "recess" and "snack time" and "computer lab" that captivated my imagination. School was going to be badass.

It was a great visit, and then Mom dropped the bomb and ruined my entire day in a single sentence: "Let's go meet the nurse now so we can teach her how to help you go potty."

Excuse me? Why would I need to potty at school? That was an activity strictly reserved for the upstairs bathroom at home, with the door closed so that nobody ever found out I peed into a red plastic pee bottle rather than the toilet. If people found out about that, they'd think I was weird, and if they thought I was weird, they wouldn't want to talk to me or be my friend. No thank you, Mother, we can skip the nurse's office.

I stopped my chair in the middle of the hallway and turned it off. My undeveloped mind expressed my opposition in a series of whiny moans.

"Stop, Shane. You can't hold it all day. It's unhealthy." And she continued to the nurse's office.

The nurse was a young blond-haired woman who could've just as easily been an angel. I didn't understand why, but as Mom lifted me onto the changing table in the nurse's private bathroom with the blue-eyed goddess closely watching her every move, it felt like my wiener rocketed right up inside my body. My face burned with embarrassment as Mom pulled off my undies and demonstrated how to angle the pee jar so that my dick went in correctly.

I wanted to evaporate, or die.

"Just make sure you wiggle the last drips off before you pull the jar away," said my mom. "We don't want any dribbles!"

The nurse put on a patronizing baby-talk voice: "Easy peasy. We are going to become best buddies, aren't we, Shane?"

Shockingly, we never became best buddies. In fact, I didn't use the bathroom once in all five years of elementary school, much to the dismay of my parents, teachers, and classroom aides. During those five years, I perfected the art of convincing

A newborn pee jar must be breastfed until it reaches maturity.

people that I just didn't need to pee, while on the inside, I was tormented by an aching bladder and the anxiety of not wanting anyone but my parents to help me pee.

My refusal to urinate anywhere but in the privacy of my home was an attempt to maintain a perception of normality in the eyes of my peers. My disease forced me to do so many activities in a slightly altered way—the teacher putting on my jacket, the physical therapists pulling me out of class twice a week, the aide attaching the tray I used on my wheelchair in place of a regular desk—that, even as a kid, I knew my classmates noticed my adaptations. Back then, you could be outcast simply for wearing the wrong shirt, so it seemed pretty logical to me that the ways I was different were very bad. I desperately needed to minimize all of my oddities if I had any hope of being accepted into the social circles at school. So I held my pee and let kids wonder how (or if) I went, rather than marching down to the nurse's office three times a day and further confirming their observations of my weirdness.

It wasn't until much later in life that my pee protocol finally backfired.

I was in eighth grade at East Hills Middle School. It was the end of the school year, and my entire class was getting excited about the highly anticipated class trip, which was happening in a few days. We were going on an all-day field trip to the Baltimore Inner Harbor, and judging by the lunchtime chatter in the cafeteria, I gathered that this would probably be the greatest day of my life.

There were a few scheduled activities, like the aquarium and an IMAX movie, but we would also have over three hours of free time to explore the harbor on our own. To a group of fourteen-year-old boys and girls, this was equivalent to telling us, "Go do bad things on a school day and don't worry about consequences." We were stoked.

Several days before the trip, my teacher stopped me after class to let me know that the school nurse was coming along on the trip and could help me pee since we'd be away until late at night. I thanked him for making that arrangement.

In my head, I immediately dismissed the idea. At that point in my life, I was only good at two things: not walking, and holding my pee. I resolved to hold it for the duration of the trip instead of facing the awkwardness of asking for help on what was supposed to be a day of nonstop revelry and debauchery.

The morning of the trip arrived, and in typical idiot-Shane fashion, I forgot about my plan and enjoyed two cups of coffee with my breakfast.

Dad dropped me off at the middle school around 6:30 a.m., and all the students were loaded onto a luxurious Greyhound bus. (The fact that it had seven-inch televisions that played grainy VHS tapes was the only reason we thought the bus was fancy, but that was enough for us.) The driver pushed aside a row of the reclining chairs to make a space for my wheelchair.

On the three-hour drive to Baltimore, I began to feel that familiar pressure in my bladder, the one that I'd gotten pretty good at ignoring. We carried on.

When we arrived in Baltimore, having watched *Night at the Museum* one and a half times, I was kicking myself about the coffee. The nurse had subtly approached me during the ride to remind me just to "holler" when I needed to pee that day. I thanked her, and in my head told her to fuck off. I was angry that she had even offered to help me in front of my friends. At this point, my closer friends knew how I went to the bathroom, but it remained an aspect of my care that made me uncomfortable. I could easily crack jokes about how I pee in a jar, but the thought of asking anyone but my parents to help with this private matter embarrassed me immensely.

Our first activity was the aquarium, where there tends to be a lot of water. Not the best environment for someone working to ignore his growing need to pee, but I did my best to enjoy the experience while silently cursing all fish for not being able to breathe air.

Next, we went to lunch with the chaperones—the Hooters was strictly off-limits, although as soon as free time arrived later in the day, half the class went directly to Hooters like they were giving out free money. My friends and I ate lunch at a small diner. I ordered a large iced tea and thought nothing of drinking most of it. My confidence was stellar.

The IMAX movie was about the plight of the American beaver, a poignant film that contained almost nothing but underwater footage. Lovely. It was at this point, mid-afternoon, when I began to question if I was going to make it. But the way I saw it, I didn't have a choice. Asking the nurse for help would be a clear demonstration of weirdness to my friends, and I didn't know if I could ever recover from such a blunder. Surely they would never see me the same way again.

Maybe if I don't wash my hair, kids will like me.

The day progressed with painful slowness. Free time turned out to be much less exciting than we expected—our options basically were the ESPN Zone or getting murdered in Camden Yards. In hindsight, it was a terrible place for a field trip. By the evening, I just wanted to be near the bus when it was time to leave so that we could get on the road as quickly as possible.

After about a hundred years, it was getting dark and finally time to leave. The bus ride home was an exercise in pain management and endurance. My bladder burned. It actually felt hot inside of me. My face and hands and armpits and inner thighs were sweating (probably my body attempting to excrete whatever unnecessary liquid it contained to make room for more urine). I was on the verge of passing out. Tunnel vision. I repeated to myself: "Holditholditholditholdit."

The bus driver must've known I was being an idiot, because he made sure to hit every single pothole on the drive home. The bouncing added a nice touch to my already delightful situation.

Despite all this, I somehow made it back to the school, but as we pulled into the parking lot and hurdled over the first speed bump, it happened.

I lost control and released my entire bladder into my pants right there on the bus. Once the floodgates had opened, it would've been suicide to try to close them. There was nothing I could do. It was the most terrifying, and embarrassing, and . . . physically satisfying feeling I've ever experienced. I kid you not: If you haven't felt the release of peeing after an all-day hold, try it just once. It's such a euphoric feeling.

Obviously, I was mortified. And wet—like, dripping wet. Like sitting in a warm puddle wet. Like just got out of the pool wet. So as we pulled up to the school, I did my best to avoid all interaction and depart from the bus with haste.

A friend approached me in the parking lot to say goodbye. He looked at my legs, confused, and asked why my jeans were soaking wet.

"Oh, I spilled a bottle of water on myself in the bus. Bye!"

When I found my dad waiting for me in the parking lot, I had a breakdown as I explained what happened. I suddenly hated myself for being so embarrassed about asking for help. Once my dad had finished laughing (which made me laugh), we got in the van and went home. He put me right into the bathtub and hosed me down to get rid of the Baltimore-sewer scent that wafted from my crotch. I was humiliated, but at least we were laughing about it. After all, what else could I do?

In bed that night, I replayed the day in my mind, checking and double-checking my memory to make sure none of my friends had figured out the embarrassing accident I had. It occurred to me that them knowing about the accident was way more embarrassing than them seeing me ask the nurse for help peeing. Perhaps it was time to try something new.

The next day I decided that enjoying an iced tea with my lunch was more important than my anxiety over what my friends might think about me peeing in the nurse's office.

And later that day, I took a risk and whispered to my friend

Mike, "Wanna help me go to the nurse?" In retrospect, it wasn't a very big risk. I mean, what kid is going to deny a genuine excuse to miss class time?

Along the way I told Mike the nurse was going to help me pee. He asked if she was going to see my dick. I said yes, but only because it's difficult not to see it when you're as large as I am. He laughed, and just like that it was over. For eight years I had been avoiding this moment for fear of being rejected, and in the end it amounted to little more than a stupid dick joke.

When I came out of the back room of the nurse's office, Mike asked, "Did she suck you off, too?"

Today, being the mature and well-adjusted adult that I am, I let everyone help me pee: family, friends, strangers. In fact, if you'd like to try it, just email me and we'll make arrangements.

Chapter 2

Ron

It was Good Friday, a day of somber reflection for millions of Americans. It was cloudy, but unseasonably warm for late March. It was midafternoon. I had the day off, as did my father, who spent his day doing quiet work around the house—laundry, organizing the garage, more laundry.

He came into our dining room, where I was enjoying a refreshing adult beverage and working on this very book. It was a lazy day. On the back patio to my left, a gathering of birds was devouring the seeds my mom had put out for them that morning.

My dad pulled the earphones off my head. "You good if I run over to Brian's to see his new bike?" he asked me.

"Yup," I said, not really listening. At the age of twenty-three, I stayed home alone quite often. Sounds reasonable, right? And yet, people always reacted with surprise when they learned that I wasn't constantly monitored by an able-bodied adult figure.

Take my grandfather, for instance, who thought my mom was joking when she first told him that some days during college I just hung out at the house alone if I didn't have classes. As long as I had my phone and some food within reach, I was perfectly content. As long as I moderated my beverage intake and avoided IMAX films about beavers, I could hold my pee for days, so that was not an issue. Still, my grandfather grumbled that I should have someone with me. In his mind, leaving a person with a disability alone was absurd, since his mind blended all disabilities together into a big jumble of helplessness.

With the right adaptations, I can be just as independent as anyone else, which is really important for me. The constant reliance on other people throughout my life has created in me a fear that I'm a burden. I occasionally feel guilty when asking for help, and the feeling can become pretty intense if I know I'm interrupting someone's schedule or activity by asking for their assistance. I can get irritated if my mom so much as interrupts my Netflix movie to ask how to turn off her Bluetooth, so I can only imagine what my family members must feel when their daily lives are routinely interrupted by my round-the-clock care: lifting me, feeding me, showering me, etc. Because of this burden complex, I look for every possible way to increase my independence and reduce how often I need to involve others in my care. I've been staying home alone since I was about fourteen, and it has never once been an issue.

So my dad left the room to get ready, and I returned to my work.

A few minutes later, I saw a figure walking slowly up the porch toward our back door. What the hell? Nobody uses our back door except me and occasionally my brother, but he was three hours away at college. There was a knock, followed shortly by the doorbell (which we installed years ago so I could get my parents' attention when I was playing outside). I couldn't physically turn my head far enough to see who it was through the glass back door.

"Uh, Dad? Someone is at the back door?" I said, hoping he hadn't left for Brian's yet.

"Who in the world . . ." said Dad as he returned to the dining room and opened the back door. "Hey, can I help you?"

The man's voice was old, but gentle. "May I come in?"

My dad hesitated, but then opened the door wider. "Sure, everything okay?"

The man didn't answer, but walked into our dining room, past my dad, and into my field of vision. His steps were slow, almost like he was deliberately taking his time. He stopped a few feet into the room and turned his head to look down at me. He was tall, with sleek white hair and expensive clothing—dress pants, Dockers, plaid button-up, and a black suit jacket.

"Do I know you?" he asked, looking at me with genuine curiosity. My initial thought was that he was one of my blog followers. I've had a few rare occasions where strangers felt it was acceptable to simply drop by my house to meet me. It's not acceptable—it's creepy 100 percent of the time. But his question didn't seem to support that theory. He was truly asking who I was.

Either that, or he was toying with me.

"I'm not sure, do I know you?" I said, trying not to let the bizarre situation influence my voice.

He laughed. Full-out chuckled to himself. Then, suddenly, he stopped and looked directly into my eyes. "No."

He said it with force, like a parent scolding a child, more of a command than a response, with a hint of anger. He walked farther into our kitchen, keeping his eyes glued on me. His arms were crossed.

My next thought was that this was a trick. Mom was constantly berating me for "sharing too much" on the internet, and I now wondered if she and Dad had put this little scare together to teach me a lesson. At the very least, this theory explained why my dad had been so quick to let the total stranger into our house. Another similar theory that flashed through my mind was that my dad had invited an old friend over and told him to mess with me just for shits.

The man stopped in our kitchen, directly in front of me now, and looked around at the fixtures. "This is a nice kitchen," he said. Then he turned his attention back to me. "Do I know you?" he asked in exactly the same tone as before.

The alcohol in my system was not helping at this point. I looked down, and my phone screen was visibly greasy from the sweat on my palms. My heart rate was beginning to climb.

"No, dude, I don't think so. Who are you?" I felt inexplicably wimpy.

Again: "No."

He laughed and walked around the table, toward me. The process repeated itself for a third time.

"Dad, what the fuck is going on?" I said, no longer hiding my growing fear.

Dad was still standing behind me, near the back door, and the way he answered both refuted my current theories and scared me more than anything else that had transpired so far: "Shane, I really have no idea." I could hear the fear in his voice as well—not exactly the best thing to hear from the only person capable of defending us.

"Sir, I think it's time for you to leave," he said.

"No." Laughter, laughter that carried a mocking quality, the way a bully laughs at his victim.

"Who are you?" I asked.

"Ron," he answered, matter-of-factly.

"Where do you live?" asked Dad.

He pointed to the southeast. "2308 Lansdale Drive."

"And what are you doing here?" asked Dad.

"No."

He pointed to a picture of me hanging on the wall and took another step toward me. "That's you right there." He was close enough to reach out and grab me.

My voice was shaking. "Dad, can you, like, do something?" It felt unreal, but I was sizing up the old man. He was at least seventy-five years old, well built, but still, he was old, and I decided my dad could easily take him on as long as the man wasn't carrying a weapon.

"Sir, you need to leave. Now."

"No."

The man turned and walked into our living room, out of my sight. Dad followed him, repeating that he needed to leave.

Frantically, I dialed 911 on my phone, but I couldn't physically lift the phone to my ear, and I didn't want to alert this possible psychopath to my actions by using speakerphone, so I simply dialed the number and flipped my phone over in my lap, hoping the responder could use call tracking to locate our house. Even as I did it, I couldn't believe I was doing it. I was either going to be the hero, or I was about to get murdered.

From the other room I heard, "This is a great living room you have here."

"Sir, please leave now. You're scaring my son." Cool, Dad. Blame the kid in the wheelchair.

"I have to leave now," said Ron, as if the idea had just struck him for the first time. I heard the front door opening. I flipped my phone over and shouted at the 911 responder everything that had just happened, but she didn't seem to understand.

"Did he physically break into your home without your consent?"

"Well . . . No, I mean . . ."—shit, that sounded bad—"my dad let him in, but he wouldn't leave!"

We went back and forth like this a few times until she

agreed to send an officer over. When the officer arrived a few minutes later, Ron was long gone. The officer—young, bored—took down our story and said he'd take a look around the neighborhood.

I was shaken up. Never in my life had I experienced a threat of physical violence. I was twenty-three years old and I had never seriously considered the fact that I couldn't defend myself. In the past ten minutes, Ron had rudely awoken me to that reality. What if I had been alone? What if his intentions really had been malicious? I was utterly defenseless! Sure, I could dial 911, but it would not be hard to take away my phone. What if he came back while I was alone?

Imagine standing in an alligator-infested swamp with your arms and legs tied. Do you feel safe?

Dad decided not to go to Brian's (thank God), and we spent much of the rest of the day attempting to replay Ron's visit in search of clues that we had missed. After dinner, I sheepishly asked my parents to reschedule their plans to meet friends for drinks. I did not want to be alone that night.

Before the family went to bed, Dad locked all of our doors for probably the first time ever. It's ironic how a locked door—ostensibly much safer than an unlocked door—can make you feel like you're in danger.

I fell asleep analyzing every tiny creak of the house.

During breakfast the next day, we discussed Ron's visit again. I was still thoroughly unsettled, thinking through all the moments I'd be alone in the coming weeks. I started texting friends and family to see if they were available for an hour here and an hour there. Many of them rearranged or altered their schedules to hang out, which caused some pangs of my burden complex, but right then I was more concerned with my safety. It felt ridiculous to be this scared by an old man, but his sinister laughter kept replaying in my head. He had been toying with me, I was sure of it.

To further protect myself, I went online and began researching home security systems.

On Monday, life returned to normal. I managed a nonprofit organization from the dining room of my house. When my co-workers, Erinn and Sarah, arrived to the Laughing at My Nightmare, Inc. office, they gave me lots of crap as I recounted the events of the weekend. To them, it sounded like instead of helping an old man with Alzheimer's who got lost and ended up at our house, I called the police and made him out to be a blood-crazed predator. As they were making fun of my neurotic, overly imaginative mind, we heard footsteps on the back porch. Ron had returned.

He approached the back door and stood there silently, his gaze fixed intently on me through the glass. Sarah went to the back door but did not open it.

Ron pointed at her foot. "That's a nice tattoo."

"This is not your house. You need to go home," Sarah said to him.

"Do I know you?" He let loose one of his signature laughs and began trying to open the back door. It was locked, but he continued to jiggle the handle with increasing frustration. My stomach was in my throat. Erinn was dialing 911 as Ron stepped off the porch and began to circle our house looking at all of our windows for a place to enter. We heard him fussing with the front door of our house, which was also locked.

The police arrived and calmly explained that they had picked him up a block away and taken him home. He indeed lived just down the street, right where he'd told us. They said this was not the first incident they'd had with him. Classic dementia, they said. Erinn and Sarah gave me a look that said, "We told you so," but this explanation did not immediately calm my nerves. I was angry and jacked up on adrenaline from fear after a potentially dangerous man had tried to infiltrate my home for the second time in four days.

I said to the cop, "He just tried to break in. You can't arrest him?"

The officer reiterated that Ron had dementia, explaining this to me in a soft, gentle voice as if the situation were beyond my comprehension. He was not dangerous, the officer assured me. "There's really nothing we can do."

Later that day, I purchased security cameras. I'd known the phrase "paradigm shift," when your view of the world suddenly changes in a profound way, like when it was discovered that the Earth revolves around the sun, but I'd never personally experienced one.

Now I had. My sense of safety was distinctly cut into two phases of my life: the time before Ron's first visit, when I was carefree and secure, and the time after, when I was extremely cautious and obsessive about not being alone. I was angry that no one else seemed to understand how unnerving it felt to suspect looming danger with no way of protecting myself.

Over the next four months, Ron came back seven more times. I'm not sure what it was about our house, but every time he wandered, he ended up at my back door. One of the times, he brought a Miller Lite with him, finished the can on our porch, and deposited the empty in our recycling bin. Another time, he stood next to my van and refused to move so that we could back out of the driveway. Eventually, I stopped calling the police, as it became clear they were not going to arrest the man for simply "trying" to break in.

Looking back two years later, I feel bad about how I handled the entire Ron ordeal. My initial fear of his going berserk and trying to eat my face was probably unwarranted, but his visits did cause a big shift in how defenseless I feel. Not being able to physically protect myself was a legitimate concern, but as Ron repeatedly tried to get inside my house, I never once attempted to understand Ron. I made assumptions about him based on his age and his clear dementia without considering his specific case. I installed security cameras rather than helping him walk home.

One of the most frustrating things about my disease is the tendency for strangers to make negative assumptions about me because of my wheelchair and appearance, like my grandfather assuming I can't be home alone. I must constantly work to overcome social stigma when people judge me by how I look. However, when I was faced with a person living with dementia—a condition I'd never come into contact with before—I rushed to make negative assumptions: He's dangerous, he's unpredictable, he's targeting me. I only thought about how his suffering negatively affected me and never truly considered his humanity. That was wrong. And hypocritical.

So, Ron, my dude, I know it has been a while since we've hung out, but I want to say I'm sorry. I'm sorry that I thought you were evil, or faking, when in reality you were dealing with a terrible condition. I hope that, wherever you are, you're receiving the care you need.

If we ever meet again, let's have a few Miller Lites together.

Chapter 3

Locked Out

Ron paid only a brief visit in my peaceful life, but his role in my story was significant and destructive. Whereas before his attempted break-ins, I was content to stay home alone for long stretches of time, after his visits I spiraled into a prolonged period of nervousness and vulnerability. Although I eventually accepted that Ron was not a threat to my safety, his mere presence brought with it the realization that I would be unable to protect myself from someone who did wish to harm me.

To fortify my defense against this newly perceived threat, I became neurotic about my safety. I went to great lengths never to be alone. When I had no option but to be alone for any stretch of time, I demanded that all doors be double locked. Instead of spending my home-alone time in my bedroom or our dining room, where I had no sight of the outdoors, I set up a new workspace near the window of our living room, which provided me an easy view of the road in front of our house. Should anything suspicious go down, at least I could watch it developing from my new position and get a jump start on calling the police. I Googled ways to booby-trap a house like I was Kevin from *Home Alone*.

Several times—and I cringe to share this with you—I panicked when I saw someone approaching the house, causing me to call my neighbors and ask them to come over and check out the situation. Every time it was embarrassing—a power-line inspector or a door-to-door salesman or no one at all—but even in my embarrassment I couldn't shake this new, intense fear of being totally susceptible to danger. (Also, I just want to give a huge thank-you to my neighbors Jim and Tess, for coming to my "rescue" every time. I appreciated that so much.)

My friends and family, although supportive of my new defensive measures, clearly did not fully understand the type of fear I was experiencing. Requests to lock the door or set up a security camera were met with jokes, and I don't blame them. They all have a built-in security blanket: They can attempt to run away from or fight off any physical threat they might encounter. I, however, felt like a sitting duck: I was stuck in my wheelchair, just waiting for someone to get into my house and harm me. No matter that the chance of this happening was infinitesimally small.

I consider myself to be a rational person (which is probably something an irrational person would say), so I recognize that

I live in a quiet suburb that probably hasn't seen an actual crime in sixty years. On top of that, I know that it would take a particularly terrible type of person to target a cute little wheelchair boy like me. But even rational people can have irrational fears. Ron had truly rattled me.

It was not until many months later that another scary experience finally forced me to relax.

Like one-seventh of all scary occurrences, it happened on a Tuesday. My parents were attending a dinner function, and I didn't want to be alone for those couple hours, so I put out some texts to friends to see if anyone was around. One of my friends, Martha, an intensive-care nurse who was visiting from Philadelphia, said she'd swing by. Our agenda for the evening included eating chicken wings that tasted like spicy cardboard and drinking beer. Just a real classy night all around.

Several hours into the evening, I needed to pee, and Martha offered to help me. Being friends with an intensive-care nurse definitely has its perks; she knew how to lift and bathroom me without much instruction, which saved us a solid three minutes every time.

After emptying the contents of my pee jar into the toilet, Martha said she was stepping outside for a cigarette, and did I want to be lifted back into my chair before she did that or was I comfortable to stay lying on my bed for the two minutes that she would be outside?

I laughed at her question and said I was fine to stay in bed.

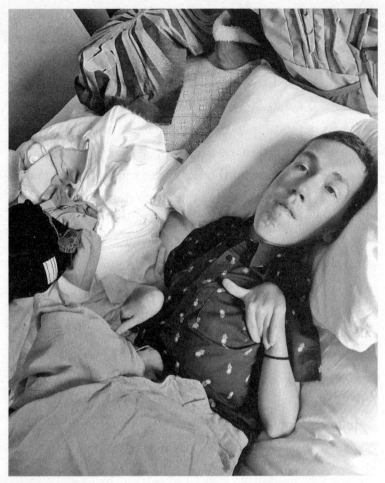

Did you know that one in every four people who use wheelchairs sleeps with their eyes open? That's a true fact that I made up.

Martha probably didn't know it because we'd only been friends for a few months, but this response was quite out of character for me.

As a child, I had developed an intense fear of being left to die in my bed. Having zero ability to move once lying down, I had trouble coping with the (incredibly unlikely) possibility that I would be abandoned by all those who care about me, and left to starve and rot in my bed until death arrived. (Okay, so maybe my Ron fears were not the first time I've been a bit irrational.)

The origin of this fear was one singular night in childhood when my parents sat on the front porch after putting me to sleep. I called for them, and they didn't hear me. So I panicked and began to scream for them, and when they still didn't rush in to rescue me, I assumed they'd been murdered and that I was now left for dead.

Considering this childhood fear, coupled with my new difficulties being alone, I still have no idea why I agreed to stay in my bed.

Martha walked outside. I heard the front door close. Minutes passed. I heard the front doorknob making noises, but no Martha. More minutes passed.

That was odd.

Then I heard my back doorknob jiggle, but no Martha.

Shit.

It dawned on me that both the front and back doors had been locked when she stepped out, a consequence of my newfound fear of intruders. Martha, not being used to the doors being set to automatically lock, had probably pulled the door closed behind her to keep out the cold, and locked herself out.

A few minutes passed, during which I imagined Martha checking every window for an unlocked entry point. She's going to figure this out, I told myself. The wind howled outside. Worst-case scenario: My parents would be home within a few hours and they would either have keys with them or would authorize the breaking of a window to get inside.

I was perfectly safe, perfectly comfortable, and yet my brain began to imagine the most horrifying of outcomes.

What if Martha tripped in the dark and was hurt and my parents received a terribly timed call from my brother, who needed them to immediately drive three hours to help him with something urgent at college? I'd be stuck there all night, and without my feeding tube at 10 p.m., my blood sugar would certainly drop. I'd fall into a coma, and because of my depressed lung function, I would obviously stop breathing. That would be the end.

Or what if I got a coughing jag and needed to puke (it doesn't matter that this has never happened, it could happen!), and I was unable to roll over onto my side? I'd vomit on my back like a volcano, aspirate, and die. Simple. Fuck, why hadn't she broken a window yet?

My heart was racing, hands dripping buckets of sweat. Then I heard her voice, faint but clear, coming from outside my bedroom window: "Shane! I'm locked out!"

"We have a spare key!" I yelled, realizing it as I yelled it.

She could hardly hear me. The wind was particularly strong that night. I repeated myself.

"Where is it?" she screamed back. Oh, to be my neighbors observing this interaction from afar.

I attempted to yell directions, but she only partially understood me, which I gathered from the growing panic in her responses. More minutes passed. Nothing. I began to accept that I was not going to survive and started making peace with everything around me. It had been a good life, mostly enjoyable, relatively pain-free, full of love and excitement. I kid now, but in that moment I was nauseous with distress.

The front door clicked open. She came down the hallway in a rush, tears in her eyes, and suddenly everything came to a screaming halt.

Time stopped.

Our laughter filled the bedroom.

She put me back in my chair. I was alive and that was all that mattered. During our celebratory adult beverage, though, I couldn't help but replay the situation in my head on repeat. Never in a million years would I have forgotten to check the lock like Martha had. It wasn't her fault; she just doesn't have a Neurotic Safety Officer in her head like I do.

In fact, no one I know thinks through situations at the same level of detail and caution that I do, because they have no reason to worry about such trivialities. For me, a locked door could mean death. Unlikely, yes, but still something I worry about.

This incident ended with laughter, but it also inspired me

to cut back on my Ron-era safety precautions. Living in a military-level safety zone was too difficult when I had to share that space with carefree people. It still scared me, but I knew I was just asking for more mishaps and stress if I continued living my life behind double-locked doors.

Chapter 4

Road Rage and Rag Dolls

After plopping out of his mother's baby-hole, an infant giraffe lies in a mangled mess of cockeyed legs and neck, squirming about in a pool of afterbirth. He's weak and has no control over his body. As time passes he must learn how to stand upright, wobbling about on spindly limbs, teetering on the brink of toppling at the slightest gust of wind.

In terms of physical appearance and strength, my body is comparable to that of a newborn giraffe, although most of the time I'm not covered in afterbirth.

Spinal muscular atrophy has worked its deteriorating magic on me for many years, to the point where my weakness is bordering on paralysis in many areas of my body.

For instance, I'm losing the ability to hold my head upright, which requires neck muscles to balance the weight of my head. This new loss of ability creates issues in places like the car for fairly obvious reasons. Put that baby giraffe in a moving vehicle and slam the brakes. What happens?

Once I lose balance of my head, I don't have the strength to lift it upright again, meaning I must wait in an awkward, uncomfortable sideways position until someone can assist me. These are the lovely quirks you get to deal with when you live with my disease.

In recent years, driving in my van has become an adventurous task. The slightest acceleration sends my head flying backward. A gentle push of the brake pedal flings it forward. I'm a helpless human rag doll.

I've suggested countless times that we just duct-tape me to the roof of the van in the fetal position, but so far, none of my friends or family have been brave enough to attempt that plan. Instead, I ask my drivers to accelerate, brake, and turn with careful caution. Once we get moving, I have no trouble staying balanced; it's just those initial changes in speed. When I'm feeling particularly tired, I wear a foam neck brace that stabilizes my head. For the most part, cautious driving and my neck brace have made it possible for me to safely ride in my van.

Driving cautiously, though, angers other drivers like you wouldn't believe.

One afternoon, as my cousin Sarah carefully accelerated from a green light, the driver behind us laid on his horn until we were up to the speed limit. Keep in mind, I don't ask my friends to drive unsafely. Sarah simply didn't gun the throttle to the floor. We rolled our eyes while the psychotic driver behind us flipped the bird and shouted obscenities inside his car.

A basic rule of driving is do not merge while taking selfies.

That is just one example, but it happens constantly. More and more often, people honk, gesture wildly, and tailgate inches behind us. My favorite move is when an angered driver flies past us on non-passing roads, usually while simultaneously laying on the horn to make us extra aware of his bunched panties.

I asked my girlfriend to take it easy turning a corner in a residential neighborhood last summer, and a man behind us screamed out his truck window at her: "Let's fucking go!" Literally screamed with a fury so hateful it was as if he was fleeing from an oncoming tidal wave and we had blocked his path by having a picnic in the middle of the road. He was enraged because we made the turn five miles per hour slower than he expected. Livid. We had completely ruined his day with our slightly slower turn. The interactions I face on the road are so abundant and ridiculous that I can't truthfully write it off as coincidence or even bad luck.

I began to wonder, why are people in such a hurry all the time? Surely, they can't all be late for an important meeting. They can't all have pregnant wives going into labor in the back seat.

I'm hesitant to attribute this anger to any misunderstanding of disability. Drivers behind me don't know there's a baby giraffe boy in the car. In fact, if I put a giant sticker on the back of my van that reads: WHEELCHAIR USER WITH NO NECK MUSCLES ONBOARD, I'm sure drivers would be more understanding.

More to that point, when people are aware of my disability, they're typically more sympathetic to my slowness. My girlfriend and I often visit New York City, a breeding ground for angry people with a vicious need to move quickly at all times. You'd think that when I take my time to slowly drive my wheelchair off the bumpy curb cut at the end of each block, the classic Impatient New Yorker would scoff and moan at having to step around me. Actually, the exact opposite is true. Complete strangers routinely slow down as I cross the street to ask if they can be of any assistance.

A more satisfying explanation came to me while eating lunch at Panera recently (and I'm just going to continue to mention Panera Bread in every book I write until they decide to hook me up with some kind of sponsorship—I'm also a huge fan of Apple products and Wendy's chicken nuggets).

I was sitting near the front door, and I watched as a woman entered, saw the line of three people at the cash register, and let out such an audible sigh of annoyance that I'm surprised she didn't melt into a puddle of disgust right there on the floor. Clearly, waiting for three people to order before her was an insulting inconvenience. I pointed this out to the friend I was eating with, and we watched with glee when the cashier informed her that they no longer carried the drink she wanted, another obvious slap in the face from a universe conspiring against her. She was cranky, and it felt so good to watch her be so cranky. I enjoyed that they didn't have her drink. Serves her right, I thought.

As the woman walked past us on her way out, I heard her say into her cell phone, "I'm on my way. Does he still have a fever?"

Oh.

Suddenly I imagined a backstory for this stranger. Sick kid. Forced to leave work to pick him up. Looming project deadlines that won't be met. Maybe no father around to help? I began to appreciate how a tiny inconvenience could lead to such outward frustration. All I had seen was a microscopic fraction of her life, but when I began to consider all the billions of details that might be at play in this woman's story, I felt ashamed of delighting in her misery. I thought the line and lack of drink served her right for being in a bad mood, but really she deserved my sympathy and understanding.

Perhaps this is the type of awareness that people are lacking when they get angry about the way my friends drive my van. Failing to realize that each and every person is living their own unique and highly complex story leads us to make assumptions that suit our own desires. People assume a slow-moving vehicle is just because of an idiotic driver, rather than considering the complicated and vast number of reasons any given car might move slowly at any moment on any given day.

I offer this idea simply because if I get honked at one more time for how we drive, I'm getting out of the van and smashing my wheelchair full-speed into the side of your precious car.

Chapter 5

Strangers Assume My Girlfriend Is My Nurse

I know it's probably tough for you to fathom, but I have had a few serious romantic relationships in my lifetime. Even more surprising may be that the women who decided to date me have done so willingly, under sound mind, body, and spirit. I didn't trick them. I didn't pay them. Our relationships were not accidents. We just fell in love.

I'm expecting your doubts about this truth because, in my experience, people generally do not naturally associate disability with romance. In my travels as a writer and motivational speaker, I've interacted with hundreds of thousands of people, and more often than not, they react with awkward shock and obvious confusion when they learn that the beautiful lady standing next to me is, in fact, my girlfriend. Let me give you an example.

A few years ago, I was dating a girl named Aruba (that's

not her real name, but how sexy would that have been?).
Aruba and I were out on a dinner date when a stranger approached us to have a friendly conversation. He said that he was a huge fan of my writing, and then turned to my girlfriend and asked, "Are you his sister?"

Now, there is nothing inherently wrong with his question, but if I saw two young people out having a nice meal together, I would probably assume that they were dating, or at least friends, and if I wasn't sure, I certainly wouldn't venture to blindly guess.

This, however, does not seem to be the assumption people make when you throw my wheelchair into the picture.

On many occasions my girlfriend was questioned about the nature of our relationship. People asked if she was my mom. People asked if she was my nurse. Once, a person blankly asked if she was "the one who takes care of him." Over time we got used to this bizarre, recurring question, and often found ways to poke fun at their ignorance.

"He's my dad," Aruba answered with deadpan perfection.

"My parents pay her to be my friend," I once said.

The mind-set that causes a stranger to automatically assume that any female in my presence is a nurse or family is one that ignores the reality that people with disabilities can and do have "normal" romantic relationships. I place normal in quotations because I'm not sure if there is such a thing as normal when it comes to love.

For a good chunk of my young life, I didn't think I was

worthy of that type of affection. I was convinced that my physical limitations would not only prevent girls from wanting to date me but also keep me from being a good boyfriend.

Here's how my teenage logic worked: I will not be able to pick her up in my car, I can't give her hugs or hold her hand very well, and we will be restricted in the activities we can do for dates. On top of that, she's almost definitely going to be a major contributor to my daily care. There's no way all these factors won't eventually become a burden for her. It all seemed rather hopeless in the heart-wrenching, hormone-fueled days of middle and high school.

I worried even more that a girl would date me out of pity, silently putting up with the annoyances of my disease because she felt bad for me. This sounds ridiculous now that I'm older, but society had thoroughly convinced me that people pitied me to such extreme degrees that a woman might fancy herself in love with me even though she felt mostly sympathy.

Then college came and I met some spectacular people who helped me shake the notion that love was only for the physically abled. It was as if my brain opened up and I began to unlearn all the things I had believed about how my disability works in the world.

Sure, I couldn't hold Aruba's hand in the traditional sense, but we made it work. (To be fair, our fingers looked like a catastrophic train wreck once they were intertwined in the precise position that I could manage, but we were holding hands!)

I couldn't pick her up in my car, but so what? She enjoyed driving, and so we made it work. I couldn't go mountain climbing with her, but I made her laugh, so we found other activities, and we made it work. And no, I couldn't jump on top of her in bed, but she could jump on top of me, and so we . . . actually, that one just worked by itself.

Once I realized that there were girls out there who were more than happy to "make it work," the fear of being unloved for all eternity drifted away like a funny joke of the past.

Today, I live with the firm belief that an able/disabled relationship can be even more satisfying than your average romance. I know I'm still young and stupid, so I don't want to pretend I have this all figured out, but I believe romantic fulfillment comes from true intimacy and that deep closeness in an able/disabled relationship blossoms from the process of teaching one partner to "care" for the other. If I were able-bodied, I might be conditioned to believe a real man doesn't show vulnerability to a woman, and it might take a while for me to open up to a girlfriend, but because of my disability I'm forced to show vulnerability right away, and our relationship is that much more intimate from the get-go.

For example, the first day that Aruba and I ever spent together, we went out for brunch at a local diner. This outing required Aruba to learn many new Shane Helper Lessons in a very brief amount of time—things like putting on my jacket, driving my van, picking up my head when I lost my balance, cutting my food, and helping me take sips of my drink.

The good news for people helping me take sips is that the slightest mistake can cause me to choke and die.

At this point in our relationship, I hardly knew Aruba, and I was afraid that I might overwhelm her with all of this Helping Stuff. I must have expressed this in some fashion, because I vividly remember a conversation where she promised that she was excited by the prospect of learning how to help me.

There is something profoundly intimate about a promise like that. On my end, I felt a deep sense of serenity from trusting her with my care. On her side, and I've checked with her, there was an important emotional connection that began to develop when she chose to be with me despite the extra requirements of needing to help cut my meatloaf.

As we began to experience life together, starting that first day at brunch, we encountered innumerable moments of humor that arose from my Shane Helper Lessons. We reveled in these moments, embracing whatever occurrence led to our fits of giggling, rather than letting awkwardness create tension in the relationship. This mutual laughter brought us even closer. In fact, one of our main sources of bonding became teaching her how to keep me alive, like how to brush my teeth without choking me, or how to put my shoes on without snapping my ankles, or how to shave my face without slicing my jugular.

That is why I got confused when strangers assumed that she wasn't my girlfriend, because to us it always seemed so normal. It was fun and it was silly and it was beautiful, and even though we didn't last forever, we never thought twice about the fact that our relationship was abnormal in any way.

We simply made it work.

Chapter 6

Buffalo

It was a Sunday in early January, and like most Sundays in January, I was urinating. My brother was the one doing the honors on that particular Sunday afternoon—lifting me to my bed, removing my pants, asking why I never shower on Sundays, and steering my dick into the red plastic pee jar. (Two out of the three books I've written so far now include a vivid description of my brother handling my penis, so that's weird.)

But this was not your typical Sunday pee session. For the past few days, a scary and exciting idea had been gnawing at my mind, and now was the moment where I was going to release it to the world, specifically to Andrew.

We had a football game on in my room, so our attention was mostly tuned to that. In retrospect, this distraction probably lessened the poignancy of the heavy conversation we were about to share.

I tried to be casual and direct. "Hey, would you want to take some kind of trip together before you go back to school?" Andrew was a junior at Lock Haven University, studying ecology. He drove three hours home every few weekends so we could hang out and watch football.

Andrew was obviously not expecting this question. "Uh, what? Where?" he asked.

"I don't care, anywhere, somewhere we both haven't been."

He shrugged in half agreement, which would've been the end of it on a normal day, but I had expected him to be neutral at first. So I continued, "I'm serious, dude. I'll cover the cost. I want to see new places and do something different than sit here playing *FIFA* for your whole winter break."

I must've sounded too forceful, because Andrew said, "Jeez, chill. Why do you want to do this so badly all of a sudden? Are you done peeing?"

I only had one chance to impress upon him how serious I was, but I also didn't want to make him uncomfortable with the truth, so in a way that only brothers can do, I skirted around the issue: "Andrew, you know exactly why. We don't need to talk about it, but we need to go do shit. Not in five years. Now."

In better moments, I know that thinking this way is absurd, but I was going through a rough phase in my life where the reality of my disease was at the forefront of my mind and made it difficult to dispel my fears—I was always getting weaker, and this decline would continue to erase my physical abilities year after year until it left me totally dependent on humans and machines just to stay alive. I was beginning to feel trapped, and I was looking for any way to prove to myself (and others) that I wouldn't let my disease restrict my freedom.

His face softened and he looked away. "I know. Okay, yeah, fuck it, where should we go?"

With that, my stream sputtered to a close.

That night, we booked a two-night stay in Buffalo, New York, for the following weekend. I still can't remember the logic that led us to Buffalo, being that it was January and both of us hated the cold, but despite the ridiculous destination, I woke up the next morning with a new excitement in my chest that I previously feared I might never feel again. I was doing something different, something unexpected, and the possibilities were endless. I felt free.

First, we had to get ready. Andrew and I have a few distinct personality differences that complicated our preparation for the trip. I am neurotic and detail-oriented to an obnoxious degree. On the other hand, Andrew can be informed that tomorrow he'll be taking over as President of the United States, and that Russia is launching a full-scale invasion, and that the Mafia is planning his assassination, and that his pants are on fire, and he'll still maintain a cool attitude of "it'll get sorted out somehow."

I wanted (no, needed) to make an extensive packing list and shop for supplies well ahead of our Thursday departure.

Andrew wanted to wake up Thursday morning, toss some shirts into a bag, and go.

My penchant for planning won out and we made a packing list, but as a symbol of his opposition, Andrew filled the list with items we didn't need: our cats, tampons, nails, etc.

The morning of the trip arrived. I ran through a mental checklist several times while Andrew scooped some clothing off his floor and stuffed it in my already-packed suitcase. It was a balmy thirty-eight degrees in Bethlehem, with much colder temperatures expected in Buffalo that weekend. Several times that morning, we questioned what we were going to do for three days in frozen upstate New York, but the "plan"

The first time Andrew sat still for more than a few seconds was well after his fifteenth birthday.

never got much further than "eat wings, swim in the hotel pool, and . . . uh, figure the rest out along the way?"

Our lack of a schedule went against the very nature of my cautious mind, but I decided that this trip would be a perfect opportunity to learn how to let go a little bit. To be fair, at the heart of my need for control and organization is fear. What happens if we arrive to our hotel six hundred miles from home and discover stairs leading to the front entrance? What happens if the parking lot is four blocks away and it's snowing? What happens if the hotel bathroom is too small for Andrew to lift me onto the toilet? My disease creates innumerable considerations that need to be properly met for me to be safe and comfortable. One unexpected narrow doorway can completely ruin an entire trip.

But there are very few people on this Earth whom I trust as much as my brother, so I decided to take the opportunity to be spontaneous—to relax and enjoy the trip as it unfolded—and accepted that the two of us could navigate any unexpected misfortunes that might arise.

Thirty minutes into the six-hour drive, we realized we forgot our bathing suits. Andrew was unfazed. "We can swim in our boxers."

That scene would thrill hotel management, but it was too late to go back, so I laughed, exhaled, and enjoyed the drive through hundreds of miles of gray, snowy landscapes.

We got to the hotel—located in city-center Buffalo between Pearl and Main Streets just minutes before nightfall. Entering the city, we had almost died as Andrew attempted to take pictures of the skyscrapers against a cream-colored sunset while steering the van with his knees.

It was blisteringly cold as we got out of the van to unload our suitcases. The valet attendant was disturbingly jovial for being outside in such dismal conditions.

"What brings you boys to Buffalo?" he asked with a smile.

"Just visiting for the hell of it!" I said.

"Any exciting plans?" he asked with a hint of sarcasm.

"We might check out Niagara Falls," I said.

He laughed. "Perfect time of year for that!"

When we got to our room, the sun was still settling down over the west end of the city in a stunning orange-pink combination. We opened a bottle of champagne that we brought from home and toasted the weekend in the cold, empty city of Buffalo, the cheerful valet attendant, and the pursuit of signature Buffalo hot wings.

It turned out that there was an iconic wing spot directly across the street from our hotel, so after we'd warmed ourselves on blueberry champagne (cool, I know), we made our way out into the frozen abyss in search of wings. We arrived at the restaurant only to discover that there were two large steps to the entrance of the building, and I didn't have a coat on. Even though I was just wearing a flimsy sweater, I told Andrew I'd be fine to wait outside while he ran in to grab us food. Holy unbelievable coldness, was I wrong. Buffalo at night in January turned out to be colder than I expected, and so while I shivered my way through a torturous fifteen minutes outside, all I could think about was how incredibly in need of assistance I must've looked to every passerby. I'm surprised people didn't stop to give me money or ask where my parents were.

Andrew came out with several containers of food, and we hightailed it back to the hotel room, arriving in a mess of sniffling, snotting, teeth-chattering hysterics. Andrew cranked the heat. We opened another bottle of blueberry champagne (I see you judging my drink preferences, please stop). My lukewarm Tater Tots dish was the warmest happiness I'd ever felt. The wings were cold and subpar.

I fell asleep that night thoroughly satisfied with my life. One of my most potent fears in life is the future. As my muscles deteriorate over time, I often worry that it will become harder and harder to live the active life I have enjoyed. I've seen people with my disease become hermits, always stuck inside, in the same place, with the same daily routine—wake, nothing, eat, nothing, TV, nothing, sleep.

The possibility of that future terrifies me, and so our trip to Buffalo was the beginning of my resistance, like a promise to myself that no matter how tough things get, no matter how worn and wasted my body becomes, I will continue exploring all this world has to offer with the people I love. Having a brother like Andrew makes a promise like that possible.

Buffalo in January was about as conducive to outdoor activities as you might imagine, but we (stupidly) didn't let that stop us. The next morning, we attempted to walk down to a central area of the city for coffee, only to give up halfway when the painful bite of subzero wind chills became too much to handle. We trudged back to our hotel room and angrily ordered twelve-dollar cups of coffee from room service before hopping in the van and driving north to Niagara Falls, where—surprise!—it was too overwhelmingly cold to be outside for more than thirty seconds. With trembling blue lips and dripping noses, we made our way up to an accessible lookout as fast as we could.

Despite the rapidly approaching hypothermia, the view was crisp and magnificent, and for a short moment I saw our trip

Trying to enjoy the frostbite.

to Buffalo for what it really was. What we were doing was idiotic. It was a waste of money. It was dangerous and at several times highly irresponsible. It was poorly planned and poorly executed (e.g., that night, we would end up driving to a Buffalo Sabres hockey game "for the hell of it!" only to discover that we'd confused the dates and the Sabres didn't actually have a game that night). It was mostly pointless. And yet, it could not have been more perfect if I made it up. I was living spontaneously.

As we stood there on the balcony that stretched out over the icy blue water hundreds of feet below, the mist of the falls burning our already-numbed faces, my brother turned to me and said, "Wherever we go on our next trip needs to be way fucking warmer."

Chapter 7

Reddit

The snap judgment that causes people to look at me and instantly feel pity is one that has been turning my cheeks red with embarrassment for most of my life.

As a young kid, before I knew better, I agreed to be a special guest on the annual MDA Labor Day Telethon, which, for those of you born after the internet was invented, was a yearly fundraising event held by the Muscular Dystrophy Association that brought in millions of dollars to fund muscular dystrophy research. It was basically a twenty-four-hour concert/comedy performance, with breaks between every act to ask the audience for donations. Until his passing, comedian Jerry Lewis was the figurehead of this nationally televised event.

Tiny little Shane wheeled out into the spotlight when it was his turn, feeling all kinds of nervous after a woman backstage insisted they put makeup on my face to "reduce the oil." I had a suit on, which felt uncomfortable and made me even more self-conscious. To top it off, I didn't really understand why I was there. I knew I was going to be on TV in front of millions of people, and that my job was to say thank you to all the people who gave money to help kids like me. I felt confident enough in my ability to say the words "Thank you!" and being on live TV had the shiny allure of something only famous people do, so I had agreed to do it and hadn't thought much more about it.

Rows of television cameras watched me drive out from a hundred different angles. An old man in a tuxedo was holding a microphone in the center of the stage. His voice reminded me of the hosts on the game shows my parents liked to watch.

"Next up we have another one of Jerry's very special kids, Shane Burcaw from Pennsylvania. Shane is eight years old and likes to play baseball," and to my surprise, a large audience hiding behind the spotlights let out an emphatic "Awww!"

What was so adorable about me playing baseball? Nobody aww'd when they learned that my little brother played baseball. Sadly, this was only the beginning of five extremely humiliating minutes.

The host gave me an exaggerated hug when I reached him, taking subtle, but careful precaution not to touch me. I noticed hair spewing from his ears.

He turned to face the camera and his voice became deeply somber, like a grief-stricken family member preparing to give a eulogy. "Why do we do these telethons every year? You're looking at our beautiful, smiling reason right here." He placed a hand on my shoulder and continued. "We raise money for kids like Shane, who live every day dreaming of a cure, who wish for nothing more than an end to their suffering, an end to their pain, who dream of running on the playground with their friends, and being free from the wheelchairs that hold them back from so much."

I stared into the bright lights and felt my face growing hot with shame. He was making it seem like I lived some awful, terrible life. I didn't spend every day wishing I could walk. I spent every day playing outside with my friends, doing homework, and being a regular kid. In fact, not being able to walk rarely crossed my mind! I did everything pretty normally, just in my wheelchair, and as far as I could tell, I was one of the happiest kids I ever knew. This old man was talking like I spent all day crying alone in my bedroom.

This was my first taste of how the world sees disability— how people assume I must live a wholly depressing, hopelessly sad existence just because I can't walk. Even worse, the man was encouraging that type of pity to get more donations! I smiled into those television cameras and said my big "Thank you!" But I didn't feel happy or thankful. Instead, I was confused and embarrassed.

As I got older, I began to better understand the tendency of society to portray disability in a negative light. It was like anything else: People didn't understand it, so therefore it must be bad. In time I developed a thick skin to this kind of misunderstanding, so that when elderly folk approached my mother in the supermarket to extend their warmest condolences to her, the sad mother of the sad child in a wheelchair— "He's a blessing in disguise," someone said to her once—I was able to laugh off these idiotic gestures and maintain my dignity. Society had it wrong, but their wrongness was so deeply ingrained from centuries of outcasting the disabled that it didn't help to get angry. Once again, it was easier just to laugh.

(Sidenote here: Forcing myself to dig through my memories in search of meaning is a truly surreal experience. I'm finding, in the writing of these chapters, that my current attitude toward the world is, indeed, traceable to concrete moments that speckled my childhood. In other words, the geriatric doofs in the supermarkets of my youth are directly responsible for turning me into the sarcastic, distrusting asshole I am today.)

In November of 2015, when I was twenty-three years old, I experienced a stark reminder that the world hadn't changed a whole lot in the fifteen years since my humiliation at the MDA Telethon.

I used to frequent a website called Reddit that described itself as "the front page of the internet." If you're unfamiliar with it, Reddit is a place where anyone can post anything— photos, personal stories, questions, news, etc.—and then anyone on Earth can view and comment and "like" the material. The "liking" feature (called "upvoting" on Reddit) acts as a ranking method for the millions of posts to the site that occur each day—an important way of sorting through the junk, since Reddit averages over a billion (with a b) visits every month. Posts that receive more upvotes from the online community have a better chance of being seen by the multitudes of daily visitors. Reddit also categorizes posts under thousands of different "subreddits," so, for instance, there is a subreddit called "Politics" that contains only posts about . . . you guessed it! Politics. Each subreddit has its own set of rules (e.g., in the "Horror Movies" subreddit, you are not allowed to post a silly picture of your niece picking a flower, unless, of course, she is also being stung in the eyeball by a hornet), and these rules are policed by moderators who are like the gatekeepers of the website. It is all very democratic and seamless.

Half of you reading are rolling your eyes right now, wondering why the hell I'm devoting three-quarters of my entire book to describing the Reddit interface. I promise, there's a reason! Reddit was about to take a massive shit on my self-esteem.

You can get famous if one of your posts gets popular on Reddit. One day, while looking through photos on my computer, I found a photo of myself with two unbearably cute kittens perched on my lap. It was from a photo shoot I had done a few years earlier, but when I saw the photo, it hit me: This picture could go viral on Reddit!

I logged into my account and contemplated which subreddit

Sexy, cute, disability . . . this photo was a winner.

this photo would perform best under. The most obvious choice, for a photo of precious baby kittens, was the "Aww" subreddit, which defines itself as "Things that make you go AWW!—like puppies, bunnies, babies, and so on . . ."

Choosing a witty, attention-grabbing title for my post would be a huge determining factor in its success, so I pondered it for a while, and then titled it, "I have an adorable disease called spinal muscular catrophy."

See what I did there? The real name of my disease is spinal

muscular atrophy. See? Atrophy. Catrophy. Because of the cats on my lap? Brilliant, I fucking know.

To my zero percent surprise, the picture started blowing up immediately. A hundred upvotes! Two hundred and fifty! Five hundred! My picture made it to the top of the "Aww" front page in like fifteen minutes, which is Redditspeak for: It was going viral. I was jubilant.

I logged out to go do something more productive with my time, and when I came back a few hours later to check if I was famous yet, the post was completely gone. I thought the site was malfunctioning. Where was it? I had been in the fast lane to fame and fortune and now my photo had completely vanished!

There was a message waiting for me in my inbox—*POST REMOVED. VIOLATION OF RULE 1.*

What the fuck?

I looked up what Rule 1 contained for this particular subreddit, and I'm not kidding here, what I read felt like a punch to the stomach.

"Rule 1: No 'sad' content, such as pics of animals that have passed away . . . or sob stories."

Apparently, in the eyes of Reddit, a site I respected for its forward-thinking embracement of all people and all ideas, simply living with my disease was considered too "sad" for inclusion on a page that was filled with thousands of able-bodied people posing with their animals.

I closed my laptop and went about my life, disheartened

once again by society's inability to see me as anything but a woeful, pitiable, dying man.

We need to change this stigma. Disability does not equal sadness. And yes, I'm mostly just mad because I didn't get famous.

Chapter 8

Laughing at Our Nightmare

Sarah nervously adjusted our notes on the make-shift podium (two wooden crates stacked on top of each other) as we waited for the audience to wander in and take their seats. The stage was constructed of hay bales with a wooden board laid atop, which had been made "wheelchair accessible" with another few pieces of plywood angled off the edge. In the field just outside this large event tent there sat a long row of horse-drawn carriages. I took a futile sip of water to wash away the dry anxiety building in my throat.

My business partner (also cousin, best friend, and hair stylist), Sarah, and I had been hired to perform one of our "motivational speeches" at a community festival near Lancaster, Pennsylvania. Normally, this would have been no big deal; our speaking careers were taking off, and we were performing several engagements every week, ranging from corporate retreats to elementary school assemblies. However, an important detail had been glazed over during the booking process for this speech, which was why we now sat in silent panic up there on the janky stage. As it turned out, we were speaking at a conservative Mennonite community festival, attended solely by devout followers of the Mennonite lifestyle and faith. Our audience, wearing traditional clothing and speaking Pennsylvania Dutch, was about to hear a dick-joke-laden presentation with a heavy emphasis on neuroscience and potty humor. A man in the front row stroked his beard and stared perplexedly at my wheelchair, waiting for us to begin. Next to him, his son pressed his nose into a Bible.

The speech began and I made a game-time decision to cut my planned opening bit that ended with the punch line, "and she said . . . turn down for what?" It was safe to assume the audience would not understand my reference to the popular DJ Snake song featuring Lil Jon. From there, the afternoon went downhill in a hurry. As we progressed through the speech, it seemed like every other joke alienated or offended the crowd before us—"We took I-78 to get here, which was super fun for my neck muscles since Sarah drives like some-one who is actively giving birth." The awkward silence was pal-pable by about three minutes into our speech. If you've ever had the opportunity to bungle a public speaking performance, you'll know the feeling of warm embarrassment that rose into our cheeks as we realized there was not going to be a dramatic recovery.

Cutting our losses, Sarah and I adjusted and began skipping entire segments that would obviously not go over well, like the part where we examine the details of a portable urinal advertisement in excruciating detail. The whole affair reached a cringing climax at the end of our hastened performance. During my closing monologue—an emotional, passionate argument for finding beauty and humor in even the most challenging situations, like a severe muscle-wasting disease—a man in the audience stood and interrupted me to share that if I'd only accept Jesus into my heart, I'd have no reason to fear death. We packed our things and left as quickly as we could.

While this experience was shocking, it was not the first time Sarah and I had been surprised onstage, and it certainly

Sarah and I enjoying some sunshine before giving a keynote presentation near Seattle.

would not be the last. When Sarah and I decided to take our nonprofit organization, Laughing at My Nightmare, Inc., from a fun, part-time side project and turn it into our professional careers, we did not know what to expect. From the moment of our company's creation in 2012, up until 2014, we'd seen a decent amount of success. In that time, through putting on random events like Halloween parties and open-mic nights, our company was able to donate a total of $17,000 to muscular dystrophy research. We were proud of this accomplishment, considering we'd created our charity with exactly zero idea of how to start or manage a charity, but after our first three years it felt like we were only scratching the surface of our potential. As 2014 drew to a close and my first book (read it, read it, read it!) was just days away from being released into the world, Sarah and I decided to meet on a cold October evening to discuss the future of Laughing at My Nightmare, Inc. This meeting turned out to be quite pivotal in the growth and success of our small company.

Two brand new ideas emerged as we sipped our mango cherrytips pesto passiondoodle tea (or whatever we ordered from Starbucks that night). First, we discussed the possibility of taking our school speaking program to the next level. Until this point, Sarah and I had actually never performed a speech together. Relying on a rotating crew of random volunteers, I had been able to book a few engagements in those first few years, but the talk I was using was poorly written (by me), and I definitely was not performing enough speeches to earn any sort of substantial funds for our nonprofit. On this night, however, we were invigorated by the idea of writing a new speech starring the two of us and dedicating ourselves to developing our presentation into a marketable service.

Okay, great, awesome, but there was an elephant sitting at the table with us. Sarah was working full-time in a sales position for another company. We could not conceive of a situation where we'd be able to expand our speaking program while Sarah was busy from 9 a.m. to 5 p.m. every day.

"I could quit," she said. She was not laughing. "Things could really take off when your book comes out. We know what we need to do to be successful—to make this our career—we just haven't pulled the trigger yet."

"What if we fail, though?" I asked. "The idea of speaking with you at a million schools a year sounds amazing, that's like my dream, to be doing that full-time, but if we fail, what will you do?"

"Worst-case scenario, I'll just get another job. LAMN is never going to become the big, awesome company that we want it to be if we don't go all in. I think now is the time."

The gears of my brain were spinning. "I have another idea!" I said. Sarah gave me a look to remind me we were in public and I was getting noisy. But my enthusiasm could not be contained. "What if," I said, "instead of giving all our money to fund research, we used it to provide equipment, like ramps and shit, to people living with muscular dystrophy? Research is important, but every nonprofit on Earth funds research. We could make a real, immediate, tangible impact on people's lives in an incredible way."

Sarah responded in three words: "Hell fucking yes."

Just like that, the wheels were set in motion for the rebirth of Laughing at My Nightmare, Inc., which officially began when Sarah left her job and joined me full-time in January 2015. Our new vision was simple: sell our service as professional motivational speakers as far and wide as physically manageable, and use the funds we earned to provide essential equipment to people living with muscular dystrophy.

Sarah turned out to be correct about my book opening up new opportunities. In fact, almost immediately after she joined the company full-time, the speaking requests started to pour in. As tens of thousands of book readers flocked to our website, they were greeted by a shiny new page advertising our availability as public speakers. It worked like a charm. Boston University called us: Can you speak for a student event? The University of Connecticut emailed: We're having an event and we need a speaker. The University of Vermont. Virginia Tech. Plus dozens of elementary, middle, and high schools up and down the east coast.

Those early days were exhilarating, but rife with the unavoidable mishaps of two young people who were doing their best to "fake it until we made it." We thought, for instance, that having the text of our presentation printed verbatim would give us confidence onstage. But when an unfortunate draft from an opened door sent our precious notes fluttering

Sarah, me, and Paul, our favorite lawyer ever. We owe so much of our success to Paul for selflessly and passionately helping us turn our idea for a nonprofit into reality.

across the floor, and an auditorium full of 250 fourth graders sat in fidgeting, awkward silence while we stammered through the rest of our talk, we learned the valuable lesson of over-learning our presentation so that we could perform it with our eyes closed.

One of our speaking highlights came just a few months later, when we were asked to give the opening keynote at a convocation for one thousand members of a nearby school district. The auditorium was massive, and the spotlight so unexpectedly blinding that for a moment I had trouble steering my wheelchair to the correct spot onstage. I managed to take my place and launch into my opening joke without plummeting to my death off the front of the stage, and better yet, the audience ate it up. Sarah, feeding off the energy in the room, improvised another joke about my awful haircut and the audience roared. We were doing it!

Back at the "office" (my house), we faced another learning curve in managing the behind-the-scenes functions of our charity. In order for LAMN to remain our full-time jobs, we basically needed to multiply our revenue by twenty. Tell any business owner to increase her revenue by 2,000 percent in one year and she'd probably quit on the spot. All at once, we had to be content creators, grant writers, donor-relationship specialists, salespeople, brand managers, fundraisers, organizational experts (still learning this one today), bookkeepers, event planners, marketing wizards, and big-picture decision makers!

My favorite "learning experience" was when I had the brilliant idea of the Laughing at My Nightmare Summer Swear Jar campaign. Trying to come up with edgy, unique ways to raise funds for our mission, I sent out a letter to fifty local business owners and managers inviting them to purchase a Swear Jar from LAMN. Every time you catch an employee swearing, they must deposit a twenty-five-cent donation into the jar. I maintain that this idea was revolutionary, a truly groundbreaking example of savvy fund-raising, but in all my excitement, I didn't think twice about titling our outreach letter, in large, bold print: "What the Fuck Is the Laughing at My Nightmare Swear Jar?"

We did not receive any responses. A few weeks later, a manager from a local bank offered to take us out to lunch to discuss our work and our mission. Sarah and I celebrated. Real, legitimate businesspeople were taking us seriously. Lunch went well, and I didn't say anything too embarrassing, when suddenly, at the very end, the bank manager put on what can only be described as his "dad voice" and sternly reprimanded us for sending out corporate mailings that contained the F-bomb—his bank had apparently been on my mailing list, and he made it very clear that my brilliant idea was not just ill-advised, but potentially damaging to our relationship with the community.

Thankfully, Sarah and I are quick on the uptake, and we settled into our new positions faster than I anticipated. Our speeches and online positivity content were booming. Every day we gained dozens of new fans and donors who wanted to support our mission. To launch the equipment-granting initiative, we gave a customized adaptive bed to a high school student living with muscular dystrophy. Once it had been delivered, the family graciously invited us to visit and see firsthand how the bed was helping the young girl regain independence. Using the handheld remote to sit herself up in bed, our recipient reported, "Being able to do homework comfortably in my bed is great, but the best part is having the ability to stay up and chat with my friends into the night."

In the three years that have passed since Sarah joined full-time, we've performed over 150 speaking engagements, from the lovely Mennonite festival, to Harvard, to biotech companies in San Francisco, to children battling life-threatening conditions in New York City. At the same time, we've raised and provided over $85,000 in equipment to people living with muscular dystrophy, from ramps to breathing devices to specialized computers. In a few months, we'll be providing a $50,000 grant to purchase a wheelchair-accessible vehicle for someone in need.

Starting out, we hardly knew what it meant to be a non-profit organization. The secret was to surround ourselves with people who did know what they were doing, to learn from them and from the mistakes we made along the way. People often ask us "What's next?" Our answer is always the same: We are just going to keep having fun, taking risks, and finding new ways to help people living with muscular dystrophy get the items they need to thrive.

Chapter 9

Jerika

In the summer of 2016, a tragic story went viral for all the wrong reasons. After it ran its fleeting course and the hoopla fizzled out, a child was dead and the disabled community had been dealt a significant blow.

The subject of the story was a fourteen-year-old girl from Appleton, Wisconsin, named Jerika Bolen. The sensational title, "Terminally Ill Wisconsin Teen Schedules Her Death and One 'Last Dance,'" caught my eye while I was surfing Facebook. I clicked the article and expected to read a story about someone with late-stage cancer or some such disease going all out for the end of their life. What I saw instead shocked me. Jerika and I shared the same diagnosis—spinal muscular atrophy type II.

Jerika was voluntarily choosing to end her life, and as I read further into the article, I realized with horror that the author was celebrating her for this decision. Not only that, but as I scanned other major media outlets, it became clear that journalists were in the midst of a fucking field day, battling each other to write the most heart-wrenching story imaginable. They called her a hero. They called her an inspiration. They put her name in lights and glorified her "wise" and "mature" nature that led her to the choice to commit suicide. All of these stories ran with a link to a crowdfunding campaign for Jerika's "Last Dance." Jerika wanted to attend a make-believe "prom" before she died, so the media did everything it could to urge readers to donate to make her dream come true.

Here's the basic story as it was being reported: Jerika lived with immense daily pain, and her mother said that they had exhausted all of her pain-management options. There was video footage of Jerika and her mother sitting in their living room with a reporter, discussing the reasons that Jerika was choosing to end her life. The pain made daily life so miserable that suicide was the only option. These interview clips were confusingly followed by shots of Jerika playing video games, smiling, laughing, and telling the reporter about her favorite hobbies, like watching YouTube and chatting with friends—all the things your average teenager loves. She appeared to have caregivers and family members who loved her and provided top-quality care. If her daily life was misery, the video footage and sound bites certainly didn't make that evident.

Writers completely glossed over the discrepancy between Jerika's seemingly—and self-reported!—good life and her desire to die. No one mentioned the fact that she was a child and that the whole situation was riddled with ethical controversy. Should Jerika, as a young teenager, be legally permitted to end her life? Should her mother be approving such a drastic measure? Which doctors were advising this decision? Instead, the media painted a grossly simplified picture: SMA is such a brutally painful and debilitating form of existence that suicide is not only logical, but commendable.

My God, did the public eat up that story. The comment sections were flooded with praise, well wishes, and prayers for her as she made this "journey to heaven." The GoFundMe page that was created for Jerika to have a special prom brought in over $36,000 as the story went viral. By ignoring all the confusing ethical questions that surrounded Jerika's decision to die, the media kept the focus on the feel-good idea of giving Jerika an amazing prom. Hundreds of friends, family, and strangers showed up to dance and cheer alongside her as she was crowned Prom Queen on the big night.

Meanwhile, much of the disability community, especially the SMA community, sat flabbergasted at their computer screens, wondering if this was all a big joke. Because the thing was, SMA (and disability in general) was being dangerously misrepresented in most of the stories that were circulating.

Many of the articles claimed that SMA Type II kills people "before they reach adolescence." This is not true. With advances in medical technology, we are living into our forties and fifties and sixties, with families and careers and passions.

Did the media mention this? Nope! They used her disease as further support for her suicide.

More articles stated that SMA Type II causes "debilitating pain." Again, not even close to true. In Jerika's specific case, it seems as if her (highly uncommon) thirty-eight surgeries in fourteen years were the cause of her immense pain. On average, people with SMA Type II do not live with severe daily pain. Did the media take the time to highlight this peculiarity? Nope! And the effect of that omission was that readers were unaware that this case was unusual, causing them to further celebrate her choice to die rather than question it.

Yes, SMA is a progressive disease, meaning that over time, I get weaker, but again, the articles used this fact to suggest that a worthwhile life requires physical ability, that life with a disability isn't worth living. Of course she wants to kill herself, the articles implied, because even without the pain, her future wouldn't be very bright. Wrong.

I know a writer with SMA who uses his voice and a lip-controlled mouse to write and is routinely published in the *New York Times*, *Los Angeles Times*, and *Chicago Tribune*.

I know a painter with SMA who has trouble lifting his arms but will blow your socks off with the art he creates.

I know a mother with SMA who is raising children and working full-time with 24–7 ventilator support.

These are the common stories of SMA: people thriving and making the most of the cards they've been dealt. I said it before, and I'll say it again: There are times when living with

SMA truly just blows. It's one hell of a disease both physically and emotionally, but the beauty in life still far outweighs the negatives for the overwhelming majority of us.

Eventually, advocacy groups got wind of Jerika's story and attempted to intervene. Their basic argument was one that many of us in the disability community were already thinking: This girl doesn't need to die—she needs help. As far as was being reported, Jerika was receiving medical advice from the doctors in her immediate area, but hadn't received other opinions before making such a drastic decision. I've found that in treating such a serious condition, more opinions almost always lead to more solutions. What might have happened if the media and the public rallied to fly her to the nation's top pain-management expert in California or Massachusetts, rather than raising thousands of dollars for her big prom?

If an able-bodied teenager went public with their decision to commit suicide because of mental illness or chronic physical pain, a GoFundMe would be set up to help them receive top-of-the-line treatment and counseling. Comment sections would be flooded with urges to reconsider. But because the prevailing story focused on the fact that Jerika's disability made her life and future so awful anyway, even without her exceptionally high pain, the movement to get Jerika more help never really gained momentum in the public eye. People were overwhelmingly content to support her decision simply because living a worthwhile life and living with a disability are not compatible ideas for a disturbing portion of the general population.

Jerika entered hospice, had her ventilator turned off, and passed away on September 22, 2016. There were no major news outlets covering her death.

Three months later, on December 23, the FDA approved the first-ever treatment to stop and even reverse the progression of SMA. It was a groundbreaking and momentous event.

Jerika was not with us to celebrate, but at least she had her prom.

Chapter 10

Beaufort

Wheelchairs and sand do not have a great relationship. If they made their relationship Facebook official, their status would be the ominously vague "It's Complicated." They're trying to be mature and work things out, but it's pretty obvious that they just aren't meant for each other. It's not hard to understand why: The electric wheelchair is a highly advanced (and expensive) piece of machinery, with hundreds of nooks and crannies that need to remain free of foreign objects in order to function properly. On the other hand, the only reason sand exists is to squirm its way into every conceivable crevice it comes across. That's why when you spend a day at the beach, you pay the price by spending the next four years picking sand out of your ears and belly button and that weird hard-to-reach spot under your balls.

Put wheelchairs and sand together and you've got a recipe for disaster.

Now, you're probably thinking: "Right, but electric wheelchairs weren't made to drive on sand. This should never even be an issue. And for someone as cautious and meticulous as you, it's even more unlikely that you would ever find yourself in a situation where you need to worry about sand destroying your wheelchair. Right, Shane?"

Here, it's important to explain that, even with my strong tendency to "play it safe," I'm still human, and therefore prone to occasional diversions from sensibility and reason. Even with a disability that forces me to consider backup plans A through Z, even while fearing that the smallest of mistakes could leave me stranded or injured, even with my belief that thoroughly planning every aspect of life is the key to success and happiness, there are still moments when all of that caution flies out the window and my careful decision-making gives way to the hedonistic urges that live inside all of us. Putting it bluntly, I can still be an idiot from time to time.

It was during one of these rare careless moments that my wheelchair was formally introduced to sand for the first time. My brother and I were on another trip a few months after our not-so-wild weekend in Buffalo. This time, we went south in search of warmer weather and crab cakes. We ended up in the town of Beaufort, South Carolina, which turned out to be quite a quaint-yet-lively little gem.

After several days of leisurely strolling the two-block "downtown" district, popping into art shops and crab shacks, and exploring the surrounding historic neighborhoods, we were hit with a sudden desire to spend some time on the beach.

Getting me onto the beach is fairly simple, assuming I have a team of eighteen Olympic athletes assisting me. I own a specialized "beach wheelchair" that is constructed with creaky PVC piping, huge inflatable rubber tires, and mesh seating. Assembling and disassembling the wheelchair (which must be done to get it in the van) takes determination, brute strength, and luck. The chair would hold a small rhinoceros, so when you plop tiny, fragile me into it, the result is plenty of room for my frail body to get tossed around. We compensate by filling this extra space with a thousand pillows. Once I'm finally locked in, I could be hit by a dump truck and not feel a thing, which is important, because pushing the damn contraption is even harder than getting it together. Pushing it over lumpy sand is a whole different monster.

Unfortunately, we had left my bulky beach wheelchair at home, a thousand miles away. This should have been the end of that idea, but the appeal of relaxing on the beach in the southern sun clouded our judgment.

We Googled the nearby beaches, and selected a state park called Hunting Island. On the way there, we were forced to think about how this beach trip was actually going to work with my wheelchair.

"So, what will I do? I can't drive on sand. If there are even tiny dunes I won't be able to see the ocean," I said.

"Maybe we can find a spot where the road gets close to the

It also floats, but I've never experimented with that feature because sharks.

water so you can stay in your chair, or I'll just carry you and lay you in the sand," Andrew said, unworried. I imagined being shit on by seagulls and eaten alive by crabs while Andrew frolicked in the water.

The drive to Hunting Island took us through a progressively more unsettling terrain of swampy wetlands that stretched our minds about the ways that real human beings live. Right in the midst of the marshes, we saw dozens of dilapidated homes set on junk-filled lawns. Children running naked, chasing each other with sticks. Old, broken cars up on their axels, dead for years. But in front of each home, near the road, painted on fresh wood in lavish reds and whites, stood a sign: SHRIMP $8/LB. I was in love.

When we got to Hunting Island State Park, there was no beach in sight, and as we drove down the single-lane gravel road, a dense forest of trees enshrouded us. It was impossible not to wonder if we were being led into a trap. The parking lot was little more than a small clearing in the middle of a jungle. As far as we could see (and hear) in every direction, there was nothing but trees and vines and wildlife and swamps.

I began to say that there would obviously not be accessible trails in a place like this, when Andrew called to me from twenty feet away, "Hey! A sidewalk!"

At this point—discovering a fully accessible trail in the most wildernessy place I'd ever been—it felt like the Universe was just handing me favors.

We followed the path into the deep, dark forest.

Pretty soon, we began to hear the familiar rumble of waves crashing. We ran along the path, trees thinning around us, and suddenly, the sidewalk ended and there was sand! Up ahead, maybe thirty yards away, was a large sand dune, and after that, we assumed, the ocean, but to get there was only a narrow path of sand that led through the last stretch of trees.

Damnit. We had come so close.

"You run up and see it, I'll hang here," I said, trying to be upbeat. My disease has a nasty way of sneaking up on me. In moments like these—traveling, exploring unencumbered, having fun—I forget about my wheelchair and my inabilities, and then I'm facing a patch of sand and it's like a switch is thrown in my head. It was all I could do not to scream. Instead, I gritted my teeth, bit the inside of my lip, and encouraged my brother to check out the ocean.

He looked around, as if a ramp might be hidden in the underbrush. "I'm not going up there unless you come," he said. (Have I mentioned that I love my brother?)

"Think I can drive on it?" I asked. To this day I don't understand why I said these words.

He laughed, and stepped into the sand to test the firmness. His shoes sunk a solid two inches as he shuffled around. "Ehh . . . Maybe if I pull you?" he said with all the confidence of a third grader being asked to perform open-heart surgery.

When you read what I did next, please remember that my need to travel comes from a deep desire to experience excitement and fear and wonder, so that when my last day on Earth arrives, whenever that ends up being, I'm not left with regret that I wasted my time here.

But you'll probably also remember that I'm just an idiot sometimes.

I inched my wheelchair off the lip of the sidewalk into the sand, with my brother holding the frame to ease the drop. I thunked down and knew right away this was never going to work. My front wheels were already a few inches deep—so deep that my back wheels (still on the sidewalk) were unable to propel me forward.

Andrew rolled up his jeans and grabbed the base of my chair, instructing me to gas it every time he gave a tug.

He pulled and my back wheels plopped down into the sand.

I tried to accelerate, but my back wheels just spun, unable to get any traction in the sand, rotating themselves into a rut. I wondered if there were dangerous animals in these woods.

Andrew yanked my chair with all of his strength, giving me just enough momentum to climb out of my wheel ruts.

"Don't stop!" he screamed.

So I didn't. With Andrew basically crawling on the ground in front of me, pulling my three-hundred-pound chair with considerable difficulty, I kept the accelerator gently pressed. We fell into a rhythm: a couple feet forward, more wheel ruts, another heroic burst of strength by Andrew, a couple feet forward, etc.

It had to look like he was dragging me to the ocean against my will.

I was sweating profusely after a few minutes, so you can imagine what Andrew looked like. We inched our way to the dune, which, thank the sweet heavens, wasn't much of a dune, but rather a cliff that looked down to the beach below.

"Get a pic of how fucked I am!"

The effort took over a half hour, and included several hang-ups where we honestly contemplated calling the police to come save us, but at last we made it to the edge, and the Atlantic Ocean came into view.

Andrew laid on his back in the sand, gasping, but besides that we were quiet for a few minutes, watching the waves break onto the beach below us.

After a long while, Andrew spoke. "I'm not pulling you back, so you're gonna have to just stay here."

Chapter 11

Rant

If you use a wheelchair and you're in the mood to be reminded just how little society thinks of you, pack your things and head to the nearest restaurant. If my experiences are any indication of the norm, your meal will include at least one insulting interaction with a stranger. If it's a particularly good night, there will also be a thick layer of awkwardness drizzled on top of your evening.

First of all, you're going to be given a kids' menu. That's pretty much a given. Regardless of your age, you use a wheelchair to get around rather than walking, so you certainly do not have the desire or capacity to eat adult foods like prime rib or oysters. Can I interest you in some apple slices or maybe a Big Boy Personal Pan Pizza with a toy? On countless occasions in my adult life, I've had to call the server back after discovering my menu had a maze and tic-tac-toe boards on it.

Now that you have the proper menu, the waitstaff has realized that you've probably been granted special permission by your caretakers to dine from the adult menu for one night and one night only. Their behavior toward you can go in one of two directions from here: either they'll embrace the charade and act like you're a competent human being, or they'll continue to anticipate your inability at every turn.

Many times, when the server arrives at my table, they'll ask whoever I'm with what I'd like to eat, instead of me. As in, I sit there looking in the waiter's eyes waiting to order while he turns to my friend and says, "What would he like?" I am not asked because it is assumed I cannot answer this question with any sort of accuracy. Waiters must fear that if they let me order, I very well might ask to sample the chandelier I saw twinkling in the lobby on my way in.

If you're interested in having an adult beverage, go ahead and forget it unless you're a masochist craving a little extra humiliation. For example, while dining with my parents one evening, I ordered a beer. The waiter chuckled, nudged my dad's shoulder, and said, "We've got a wild man!" I had to repeat my order for him to realize I actually wanted a beer. He looked to my parents with such grave concern it was like I requested that he urinate in my face. On a separate occasion, I was brought the nonalcoholic version of the vodka and club that I had ordered, and I would've thought it was a simple mistake had he not given a sly wink to my brother before he said to me, "We made it extra special for you, bud."

On the slim chance that the restaurant staff doesn't insult you, there's still plenty of opportunity to be degraded by the other patrons dining in your proximity.

Once, in my preteen years, I was watching a football game at a pizza shop with my brother. We were chanting, carrying on, and yelling at the television like obnoxious idiots. A man approached with his wife and kids. He sat down at our table wearing an expression like he just had to euthanize our grandmother and he was here to tell us the sad news.

With a voice that matched his solemn face, he said, "Do you boys like hockey?"

We nodded at the possible murderer.

"You brought me great joy tonight, seeing your smiling faces." He pulled four box-seat Flyers tickets out of his fucking pocket and put them on the table, touched my shoulder the way one does when bidding farewell to a lover, smiled, and walked away with his family.

Receiving gifts from strangers has always been a theme in my life, and while it may appear wholesome and like a pretty great wheelchair perk on the surface, it actually feels pretty messed up to me. Strangers have handed me actual cash more times than I can count, with no explanation other than a smile and some kind words about what a blessing I am. Their reasoning is clearly implied, though: "Your life must be sad and unfortunate. I can't take away your disability, but hopefully this gift will make that hardship easier for you."

Being given a gift by a stranger once or twice in a lifetime would be sweet, a neat event to write home about, but when it happens a few times a year, it forces me to confront the fact that people see my life as having such little value that they'll happily give me free stuff in an effort to "help."

My favorite interactions are the ones that mix insulting and truly bizarre behavior. One time I was out to dinner with my girlfriend, Hannah, at one of our favorite seafood restaurants, a cozy, quiet place where conversations are had over candlelight. We were talking and laughing when a woman in her thirties approached the table. She leaned toward us, placed both her hands on her heart, and said, somewhat theatrically, "You two are going to make me cry. This is beautiful." I don't need to explain why this one was inappropriate, right? We blinked at her until she went away.

A few weeks later I was having lunch at a diner when a woman came up to my table, put her hand on my neck, bowed her head, closed her eyes, and began to pray: "Lord, I ask that you heal this child of his suffering and provide him with a happy life."

Again, I was sitting with Hannah. We'd spent the morning walking along a river and visiting an antique bookstore.

"I actually live a pretty awesome life. Thank you, ma'am," I said.

Her eyes grew wide with the shock that I could speak, and she backed away muttering apologies for making assumptions. This was a relatively good outcome. I've been involuntarily prayed upon many times, but it's not too often that one of my healers realizes they've made a mistake like this.

On the one hand, these social interactions are infuriating. The constant toddler treatment makes it difficult to see myself with any sort of value in the context of society. I know in my head that I'm a funny, charismatic, intelligent, well-adjusted dude, with friends and responsibilities and goals and skills—a human—and yet, that self-knowledge doesn't hold much weight when strangers are consistently reminding me that they see me in a much different light. It would be one thing if these interactions were rare, but they happen so often that it's remarkable if I eat out and *don't* experience some form of this mistreatment. And I've only shared interactions from eating at restaurants, but this kind of treatment extends to almost every aspect of my life. The combined effect is over-whelming, an unavoidable message that I am worth nothing more than pity, and I find it extremely disheartening.

On the other hand, I was paid a buttload of money to write a book about it, so I guess I win?

Chapter 12

Deadly Ducks and Cheese Curds

Lake Harriet, one of the dozens of picturesque lakes that dimple the suburbs of southern Minneapolis, is circled by a busy walking and biking path that leads to a popular lakeside restaurant called Bread & Pickle. The area is frequented by an odd assortment of generic families of four pretending to enjoy Family Activity Time, and mustached hipsters wearing child-size cycling shorts and backpacks with nothing in them. The shady walking path is lined with benches where couples rest and enjoy the calm scene of sailboats gliding across sunny water. Three years ago, if you had told me that Lake Harriet, located one thousand miles away from my home in Pennsylvania, would someday be one of my favorite places to spend an afternoon, I would have laughingly dismissed you as absurd.

The course of my life was drastically altered by an email from a girl named Hannah in March of 2016. She was a college student (and a varsity swimmer) at a prestigious liberal arts school in Minnesota and, during a late-night YouTube binge, Hannah had come across the *My Last Days* documentary about my life—the one where I get a tattoo and talk about my penis way too much. In an effort to further avoid her growing list of assignments and responsibilities, Hannah did some online stalking and got my email address (which isn't too hard to find) and sent me a message introducing herself. As I read it, I was filled with a strong compulsion to know everything about her. She complimented my sense of humor and talked about some of the interests that we have in common, like swimming, traveling, and playing with puppies. She made fun of herself for being a creepy internet stranger and sent a link to her Facebook page so that I could see for myself that she wasn't an old man.

But what stood out about her message to me was that at no point did she call me inspiring or commend me for living with such a horrid disease. In fact, Hannah didn't even mention my wheelchair or my disability at all! In about eighteen sentences, what she did do was thoroughly captivate me with her mind and her personality. When I looked at her Facebook page and discovered that she was a tall, stunningly beautiful goddess with deep blue eyes and the sculpted body of an Olympic swimmer, it was like icing upon a delicious cake that didn't even need icing in the first place.

I emailed her back right away, and we struck up a conversation. Emailing very quickly led to texting, which very quickly led to FaceTiming, which very quickly led to shifting our daily lives around to make room for more FaceTiming. Those first few weeks felt effortless and exciting as we learned everything we could about each other. I had communicated with other girls online, but never before had it taken such effort for me to say goodbye and hang up at night. I could see that I was falling in love.

Hours of blissful FaceTiming very quickly became not nearly enough, so we eagerly booked the first of many flights for Hannah to visit in person. When I held her hand a few weeks later at an empty hibachi restaurant in Philadelphia, I realized I never wanted to leave her side. We lay awake that first night enjoying the profound difference between a computer screen and actually touching. In the morning, with my stomach in my throat, I asked her to be my girlfriend. She said yes, and we set off for a jam-packed day of activities that included a picnic in a state park because I'm the cutest boyfriend. Saying goodbye in the airport at the end of that first week was harder than all the previous FaceTime goodbyes combined. I'm man enough to say we both cried. That night, over FaceTime once again, we booked a flight for visit number two.

Early on in our relationship, I went to Minnesota to spend time with Hannah and her family. Hannah was excited to show me her home, and one of the activities we were looking forward to was a romantic stroll on the walking path around Lake Harriet, followed by a meal at the lakeside cafe. According to Hannah, Bread & Pickle served superb cheese curds, which I was dying to try while in the Midwest.

When we awoke on the morning of our lake date, the sun was shining in the bedroom window with almost artificial perfection, and Hannah was miraculously able to find a clean pair of boxers in my suitcase. It was shaping up to be a great day.

Hannah helped dress me in my sexiest lake-appropriate attire: tight salmon chino shorts and a classy button-up with palm trees on it (purchased from the children's section of Target). She carried me downstairs and put me in my wheelchair. Once there, I drove to the bathroom where I instructed her with meticulous detail how to style my disheveled nighttime hair.

"It's really important that you look handsome for all the women that you need to be impressing today," she said sarcastically.

When we arrived at the lake later that day, we discovered that because of construction, handicap access to the walking path had been temporarily moved about ninety-seven miles down the road. Our romantic walk would have to take place in the street as we searched for another wheelchair curb cut. Thankfully, we still weren't far from the edge of the lake, so we quickly forgot about the annoyance and enjoyed the view.

Not long into our walk, we passed a family dragging an unenthused toddler toward the duck feeding area. As the child caught sight of me, his jaw dropped as if he'd seen an elephant stepping on cars and blowing fireworks out of its butt. He stopped walking, shook his hand out of his mother's grasp, pointed at me, and began to shout, "Look, Mom! It's a baby! It's a baby! It's a baby!"

We smiled and did our best to ignore his shrieking, which was tough considering we were close enough to reach out and touch them as we walked past. Meanwhile, the mother was frantically trying to suffocate her child into submission.

Once we were clear of the family, the silence between Hannah and I was palpable while we waited to see how the other one was going to handle what had just happened.

"I hope a duck eats him in front of his parents," I said, and we both began to laugh.

When I was a kid, just a few years older than the shrieking toddler, I often received this same kind of unwanted attention. My classmates in elementary school zeroed in on my wheelchair specifically, since many of them had never seen a device like it before. Kids asked, "Why do you have that?" or "Where did you get that?" or "Why can't you get out of that?"

These questions cut deep, not because I was ashamed of the chair, but because I was aware that other kids viewed me and my chair as different. I didn't want to be different. The different kids didn't get invited to sleepovers. The different kids played alone on the playground.

My sense of humor was thus born out of necessity, as a way to overcome that first social barrier created by my wheelchair.

"Oh, I bought it at Kmart. I don't actually need it, but I get to leave class early for lunch, so I use it." Many kids didn't quite understand sarcasm yet, but at least they heard me talking sensibly and saw me laughing, and so they began to learn that Shane and His Chair were not off-limits. We could interact and it was cool.

In middle school, my body stopped growing as my muscles began to deteriorate: one of the lovely characteristics of my disease. Unfortunately, my head never got that memo, so as my head continued to develop normally, I started to resemble a caricature drawing. Now I had to contend with the wheelchair plus a disproportionately large head for the tiny, atrophied body.

Middle school was a rough time, and it taught me the tough lesson that I was responsible for making others feel comfortable around my strangeness. The big head thing was an unspoken insecurity of mine for many years, which further solidified my reliance on humor as a diversionary tactic. If I was out with a group of friends and someone asked why I had such a big head, it was much more socially beneficial for me to say, "My parents dropped me a lot," than to show my true embarrassment. Humor helped me cope.

In high school, my weight plummeted as my body lost the ability to eat a sufficient number of calories in a day. While everyone around me was hitting puberty hyperdrive and rocketing upward and outward, I fluctuated between fifty to sixty pounds for most of high school. My arms were twigs.

My legs looked skeletal. It was bordering on grotesque, and that's *my* perspective, so I can't imagine what other people thought.

Again (I hope you're seeing a theme here), humor was my solution. In any social situation, I fully expected strangers to react with aversion to my physical appearance, which now included a trifecta of things that made me "different"—wheelchair, big head, skinny limbs—so I learned how to disarm their awkwardness with jokes and self-deprecation.

"My parents don't feed me because they wanted a kid who could walk."

As I got older, my humor took on a shocking quality in order to take the attention off my appearance. I find that humor happens when we are confronted with the unexpected, and so the unexpected became my regular mode of expression.

Now in my twenties, my humor can get pretty dark (hence the "kid getting eaten by ducks" joke), but luckily my diversionary humor had worked once again, so Hannah and I were both still cheerful and enjoying the day when we arrived at the cafe on the edge of Lake Harriet. We navigated through the courtyard swarming with people and joined the long line to order our cheese curds. I automatically scanned the adjacent pavilion for a secluded table.

My issues with eating began in eighth grade, when my mouth suddenly stopped working during lunch in the school cafeteria. I was mid-bite on a massive beef burrito when my mouth simply failed to function. I had to spit everything out onto the plastic tray in front of me before I choked. It was like a volcanic explosion of sour cream and cheese and spit. My friends looked at me with shock and disgust. In my embarrassment, I muttered something about choking and tried to laugh it off.

It didn't go away though, and over the next few months, I found myself repeatedly unable to chew the food in my mouth.

I adapted. By jamming my wrists under my jaw like a wedge, I was able to assist my mouth with the chewing motion. My deformed kangaroo pose worked great for many years, but during that summer at the lake with Hannah, I was beginning to lose the strength for that as well.

I was hoping to find a secluded table so that Hannah could help me eat our cheese curds without awkward stares from nearby tables. To my dismay, no such table was available, so we settled for one right smack-dab in the middle of the main pavilion.

I sheepishly asked Hannah if she would mind holding my arm up while I chewed my food. She, of course, was happy to help. Immediately, almost involuntarily, I began to fire off jokes.

"It's gonna be dinner and a show for all these people who get to watch the sick boy eat cheese curds," I said. "They're probably assuming this is the first time I've ever been out of my house. You should move to the other side of the table, make it look like you're refusing to feed me. Put a fork in my hand and scream, 'Hold it!'"

Hannah laughed along with me, which was reassuring, but my head was filled with the emotional baggage of my past: of being looked at like a diseased alien creature; of being avoided on the playground; of being spoken to slowly; of being ignored and left out; of being treated differently, simply because I look different. Half of me expected her to stand up and run away at any moment.

"You know I don't think this is weird, right?" Hannah's voice caught me off guard and pulled me out of my deluge of painful thoughts. "Helping you chew like this? I don't care if people are staring. I love helping you."

Hannah and I enjoying an afternoon by the lake.

I took a deep breath, exhaled, and felt a smile grow across my face. I hadn't realized it, but the constant facade of humor was downright exhausting. Hearing her tell me I didn't need to keep up the act just for her was like sinking into a cozy bed at the end of a long day. The rest of the pavilion melted away and all that remained was Hannah, smiling at me, and forking another cheese curd into my mouth.

Chapter 13

The Elevator

In my early twenties, I went through a rough patch where living with my parents began to wear on my nerves. I can't stress this enough: My discontent really had nothing to do with my parents themselves. My parents are outstanding people who have shown me nothing but love and support throughout my entire life. Since they were my full-time caregivers, our relationship was naturally much closer than what the average twenty-three-year-old shares with his parents, but even outside of the caregiving dynamic, we have always gotten along well as a family. In fact, up to this point, I rarely thought negatively about my situation of living with my parents; it just wasn't a big deal.

But after I graduated from college, most of my friends got their own apartments, leaving for places like New York City and Philadelphia in search of jobs and excitement. My social media feed became a constant reminder of the adventures they were living, out there in the wild cities, living paycheck to paycheck but having a blast as they learned how to be adults on their own.

My friends' departure from their childhood nests prompted me to examine my own situation: I was still living with my parents and had no plans for moving out. As soon as I began paying attention to my surroundings, things that never bothered me became extremely frustrating. For instance, I had always adjusted my schedule to compromise with my parents. If I wanted to stay up writing until 3 a.m., but Dad (who puts me in bed) wanted to be in bed by 10 p.m. because he had to get up for work, then we'd discuss it and typically settle on something like 11 p.m. These types of compromises were never an issue. They made sense, and I had no problem giving up a little independence for the people who so gladly cared for me 24–7 for twenty-three years.

But as I entered this new rough patch, the compromises started to anger me. If I wanted to visit my girlfriend until midnight, or if I wanted to have friends over for a party, I should be able to do that. I was an adult with a life and career of my own, but you can't just do whatever you damn please when you're living with your parents, especially when they are the ones performing almost every aspect of your daily care from sunup to sundown. Plus, I care about their well-being, so I couldn't in good conscience stray from the mild lifestyle that we'd negotiated. You'll recall that my constant need for their assistance created a burden complex in my mind, so

I took extra caution not to exploit their obligation to care for me.

Our house itself was also contributing to the problem. We lived in a smallish ranch house. When I began wanting some separation from my parents, I realized how impossible that would be in this house. There was no privacy. Someone talking on the phone in one end of the house could easily be heard at the farthest point away in the other end, even with doors closed. So much for phone sex.

But seriously, more and more often, I found myself going outside to talk to my girlfriend on the phone. When friends came over after 9 p.m., we had to whisper in my bedroom, since my parents were getting settled into bed in their room ten feet away. Needless to say, friends stopped coming over in the evening.

I felt stuck.

Well then move out, you idiot. You're not the first person with a disability to reach adulthood, and your parents aren't going to take care of you forever, so what are you waiting for, you privileged little shit?

Unfortunately, it wasn't that simple. Living on my own meant finding round-the-clock care—someone to get me out of bed and shower me and get me dressed and brush my teeth and help me pee and hand me my laptop and get me food and help me pee again and adjust my positioning because I'm uncomfortable and get me lunch and put my coat on and take me to a meeting and bring me home and get me food and hand me my laptop and do my laundry and take the garbage out and help me poop and wipe my butt and put my feeding tube in and put me in bed and roll me overnight and adjust me in bed when I'm uncomfortable and on and on and on. It's a lot.

At that time, those duties (and I've only named a fraction of the things I might need help with on any typical day) were divided among my parents, my coworkers at Laughing at My Nightmare, my brother when he was home, my friends, and my girlfriend when she was able. It was a beautiful care system.

But that system wouldn't transfer to living by myself. I'd need to hire professional caregivers, a common experience for people with disabilities living independently, and caregivers are crazy expensive, especially when they're needed 24–7. Some rough math for you: even if I was only paying them a paltry $12 an hour, that's approximately $105,000 for 365 days of care.

But Shane, don't they have government programs and waivers and such to pay for your caregivers?

Yup! But I had made "too much" money in the writing of my books, so I didn't qualify for those types of benefits. I imagine a few of you are now grumbling about paying for it myself if I had so much money, but I promise you, the government's idea of "too much," and a realistic idea of "too much," are very different numbers. Sure, I could have blown my entire savings on caregivers for at least a few months. But could I cover rent? I'm not sure. What would happen after the first year when I ran out of money? Even if I did qualify for government assistance, I'd never be able to write another book or advance my career as a writer and nonprofit executive because I'd risk losing those benefits. That felt counterintuitive, and not worth it.

I'm sure there were work-arounds. I'm sure there were options of which I was unaware, but this brings me to the last hurdle in the moving-out dilemma: fear.

I wasn't ready to be taken care of by strangers yet. Trust is a vital aspect of the caregiving relationship for me, and because of that, I've always been cautious about who I let into that role. If I moved out, it would be a never-ending parade of random employees helping with the most intimate parts of my life. In a situation like that, I reasoned, I was only one apathetic employee away from death. I know it's absurd. I know that caregivers don't routinely let their patients die, but when contrasted with the level of trust I had in my parents, there was really no contest.

I desperately wanted to be on my own, but the fear of doing so kept me from exploring it.

So there I was, feeling stuck, and growing more resentful of my parents with every day that passed, even though it wasn't their fault. There had to be a solution.

During work one day, Sarah went down to our basement to retrieve some LAMN merchandise that she needed to ship to a customer. She came upstairs and made a joke about building an office down there so she didn't need to climb the flight of stairs every time she needed merch.

All at once, a solution to my growing misery popped into my head like a flame igniting. I almost yelled at her, "Sarah! What if I put in an elevator?!"

She was confused. "What? No. I was joking."

But now my mind was racing. Our basement spanned the entire length of our house. It was unfinished, so we used it for storage. I'd never even been down there since the only way down was a long flight of ten steep stairs.

What if I could get an elevator installed? I could finish a room down there for myself! With a bed and couches and a desk and a TV! I could have people over without needing to walk around on eggshells! I could write in private! I could even sleep down there when my girlfriend or brother was around to take care of me overnight! It would be like my own apartment!

That idea kicked off what became a six-month process of getting an elevator and finishing my basement. It began with having a few contractors come to the house to give me quotes for the work. My parents were supportive of my basement idea, and since it was my money and eventually my room, they allowed me to deal with the contractors on my own, which was initially terrifying. Each person who came was noticeably flabbergasted to learn that I was the one having this work done, and it took a little persistence to get them to address me rather than my parents as they made comments and suggestions.

As the quotes came in, the project almost came to a

permanent halt. The elevator was going to be much more expensive than I had imagined. Going into the process, I'd made a budget of what I could safely spend, and the quotes were blowing it out of the water. I became discouraged. Maybe it was just not realistic for me to be independent at that point in my life.

And then, three days before Christmas, I received a life-changing email. It was from a man named Lee Butz, who was the board chairman of a very large construction company named Alvin H. Butz, Inc. Lee had been a follower of my blog and nonprofit for a few years, and although I'd never spoken with him, I knew he was a big supporter. Lee's email was short and sweet: "Hey Shane, I heard about your elevator budget. My company will do the project for that amount. Why? Because it makes me smile!"

Lee was giving me an incredibly generous discount, one that opened up my world and increased my independence. I will never be able to adequately thank Lee and his company, but I'm hoping this chapter serves as a permanent testimony of my appreciation.

The construction began! We selected my bedroom for the elevator shaft, so for a few weeks there was a massive hole in my floor. It worked nicely as an execution pit of death until the elevator was installed.

For a few weeks, the LAMN office (upstairs in our dining room), saw a steady stream of contractors. Each day we enjoyed new sounds while we worked: drilling, hammering,

Looking down into the depths of hell.

sawing, occasional cursing when mistakes were made. The lead contractor, a man named Phil, always stopped by to see how I was doing. On the last day of the project, he made a donation to our charity. Phil, love you, dude.

My maiden journey in the elevator was exhilarating, and even emotional. The construction foreman opened the door

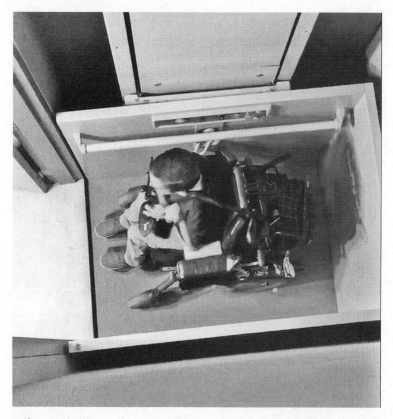

Unfortunately, they accidentally installed a one-way elevator, so I'm stuck down here forever.

when I arrived on the basement floor, and I exited into a place that I'd been living above for over fifteen years, but had never seen. I got teary-eyed as I drove around my basement, imagining the space I could create for myself down there.

Fast-forward about a year. I'm writing this in my room in the basement, which has earned itself several names already:

The Elegant Man-Cave, The Sex Dungeon, The Writing Den, and Burcaw's Basement Resort and Lodge. Behind me, on the couch, Hannah is reading. We're listening to jazz. The lights are soft and the room is warm. I don't know if I could be any happier than this.

Chapter 14

San Francisco

When I was seven years old, just months before I had a massive spinal fusion surgery to correct my severely worsening scoliosis, the Make-A-Wish Foundation granted me a Wish, and with all the sage wisdom of a small child, I decided that Disney World was the one place on Earth that I needed to go.

Arrangements were made for my family to fly from Bethlehem to Orlando, and the prospect of flying in an airplane quickly became the activity that excited me most about the trip. Minnie Mouse held no weight to the thrill of soaring through the sky at a million miles per hour.

On the day of our departure, I felt like royalty when a limousine picked us up from our house, and my little brother and I were served grape juice in champagne glasses on our way to the airport. The driver called me "Sir," and I called him "Sir" in return, letting the word roll off my tongue with grandeur. I was a king living a life of luxury.

Our local airport must have been privy to my Wish, because we were showered with Disney-themed gifts upon our arrival. We were celebrities. We were so important.

I gawked at the beautiful flight attendants, who complimented my Star Wars shirt and remarked upon my handsome good looks. They unfolded a little stroller for my parents to maneuver so that I could be wheeled on board while my wheelchair was taken below to be stored in the underbelly of the airplane. The pilot greeted me, and I was invited to check out the cockpit, a dazzling display of lights and buttons and levers and switches. By this point, I would not have been surprised if he had asked me to fly the damn plane. After all, I was no longer the regular kid I had been an hour earlier. I was big, and important, and respected.

Once Mom seat belted me into the airline chair next to her, she took a packet of Chiclets mini gum from her purse, and instructed me to chew a piece carefully upon liftoff to help with the ear popping that might occur. Normally, this warning would have terrified me, but Famous Shane Who Flies in Airplanes was not afraid of anything.

In the air, I watched the clouds pass below us with unending awe. When we landed in Orlando, a flight attendant brought me a special "Welcome to Disney" basket and asked my mom if we minded waiting in our seats while my wheelchair was brought up from below.

Many minutes passed after the rest of the passengers emptied from the cabin, but still no sign of my wheelchair. We were probably awaiting the arrival of our next limo, I assumed. Or perhaps Mickey would be welcoming us in person. Anything and everything was possible now.

Dad eventually decided enough was enough and walked to the front of the plane in search of answers. When he returned, he was red-faced. "Let's go, we need to get off."

"Oh, no, they told us to wait here for the chair," my mom corrected.

Angrily, Dad said, "No, the chair is here. It's sitting in fifty pieces at the entrance of the plane." My stomach dropped. My chair was in pieces? Was it broken? My chair was my legs. I could not possibly do a week in Disney without my wheelchair.

In the Jetway outside the plane's door, several stammering ground crew employees tried in vain to fit together an explanation as to why my wheelchair had been entirely disassembled. Their final answer amounted to little more than an embarrassed, "It's protocol . . . we think?"

Unfortunately, and ridiculously, no one knew how to put my chair back together again. The exciting feeling of being famous and important evaporated as my dad struggled awkwardly to put my chair back together.

It took an hour, but with the assistance of the pilot, we eventually got my chair into working order and continued on our way. The fun of Disney overshadowed this negative moment, but it was still a rude awakening for my young mind. An airline could destroy my wheelchair and leave me stranded, yet ultimately pay no price for the mistreatment. I didn't know it then, but what I had just gone through was actually a disturbingly common experience for people with disabilities.

Since the passage of the Americans with Disabilities Act (ADA) in 1990, it is basically illegal to discriminate against people with disabilities. But I think many people have actually turned a blind eye to the immense societal boundaries and injustices that still exist for me and my disabilibrothers and sisters (like that?). So often, when I mention that I can't access areas of my college because of steps, or that I can't afford to pay caregivers, or that flying is dangerous for me, I'm met with the confused response of, "But doesn't the ADA make that illegal?" Sometimes the answer is "Yes," and sometimes it's "No," but almost every time the answer is, "It doesn't really matter. It's still happening." People don't realize that the ADA did not immediately make the world a perfect place for people with disabilities. Far from it, actually.

Many years after my Disney Wish, I was establishing myself as a public speaker through Laughing at My Nightmare, Inc. Every week, Sarah and I received dozens of requests to speak all over the country, but we were forced to turn down many of the engagements that were not within driving distance. I had not flown since I was seven, and the idea of doing so felt impossible.

Airlines, although required to provide fair and equal access to their services to all people, regardless of disability, simply don't. For instance, I am unable to sit upright unassisted in a standard airline chair, but protocol still dictates that all electric wheelchairs be stored beneath the plane. I've called various airlines to ask what my options are, and the two I've been provided are: 1) Buy six seats on the flight and travel in a hospital bed—with medical professionals required, whom I'd need to hire, or 2) Don't fly.

Since I can't quite afford to pay $9,000 every time I fly, option two has always been preferable.

For wheelchair users who can sit in a standard airplane seat, flying means rolling the dice on whether or not their wheelchair will be returned to them in working condition upon arriving at their destination. An unconscionable amount of the time, it does not. Electric wheelchairs are complicated and fragile and extremely expensive, but those facts don't mean shit to airport ground crews, whose job is simply to put all luggage onto the plane as quickly as possible. I've spoken to dozens of individuals who braved the skies only to be told their wheelchairs had been smashed, mangled, or even lost during the flight. There are protocols for compensating victims of this type of mistreatment, but they are lengthy and impractical. How is an individual expected to effectively advocate for their justice when they land a thousand miles from home to discover that their only means of mobility has been destroyed? I read a story once of a girl who was forced to lie on her back on the plastic seats at an airport gate in Germany for several hours before her wheelchair was returned to her. Fun vacation!

So in 2015 when Laughing at My Nightmare, Inc. received a call from Genentech, a pharmaceutical company, saying they had read my book and were wondering if there was any chance I could travel to San Francisco to present to their group of SMA researchers, I explained how difficult air travel was for me. I told them I'd talk it over with my team because it sounded like an amazing opportunity, but I didn't want to get their hopes up. Since the Disney trip when I was seven, my body had become much weaker, and I couldn't imagine how I'd ever manage a six-hour flight with no way of sitting safely upright.

But as I discussed the opportunity with coworkers and friends, it became obvious that if I wanted to have a speaking career and continue growing Laughing At My Nightmare, Inc., I was going to have to solve the flying dilemma. And in order to do that, I needed to take some risks. So I called Genentech back: "I'm not sure how we're going to make it happen, but I'm in."

My coworkers and I began by tirelessly researching secrets for flying with an electric wheelchair. Sarah made many long calls to the airline to ensure that we clearly understood every detail before we left. I read countless websites and talked to dozens of individuals with SMA who had flown before. We asked my dad and my girlfriend at the time to come along and assist with the journey. Three "caregivers" may have been overkill, but I wanted to be safe rather than sorry.

We bought a child's car seat to help me sit in the airline chair. My girlfriend customized it (like a mad scientist) so that it was actually bearable to sit in for six hours. We bought a neck brace for turbulence. Dad taught himself how to completely disassemble and reassemble my wheelchair, in case of the all-too-common damage by the airline.

Slowly it dawned on me: This was possible. It would be challenging and stressful and scary, but with enough preparation, we could at least assure ourselves that it would be (mostly) safe.

On the morning of our departure, our plane lifted off the runway, and my body was pushed against the seat back by the force of the jet engines propelling us forward. I don't know if I've ever smiled as big as I did as I watched the world get small outside of the cabin window, buildings and cars becoming tiny specks of color as we floated into the clouds. I thought back to my first flight to Disney and how fancy I had felt.

Landing was just as much fun. With my dad's arm across my chest, and Sarah's hand on my forehead, I let out a nervous laugh as we touched down and the powerful brakes slammed us to a halt. We had made it.

There was a brief moment of terror as we watched from our window while the ground crew unloaded my chair from cargo storage below the cabin, desperately hoping they wouldn't drop the $25,000 piece of equipment. To our collective relief, they returned my precious baby to me in one piece.

San Francisco was like a dream. In three days we did more sightseeing than I believed was humanly possible. I drove my

How many ground crew members does it take to drop a wheelchair?

wheelchair across the Golden Gate Bridge. We plunged down the terrifyingly steep Lombard Street. I spent an entire afternoon exploring the redwood forests just north of the city. Best of all, our presentations at Genentech went perfectly, and we made some awesome connections with their SMA team.

When the idea for this trip first came up, I never imagined I'd be able to do it. Too many things could go wrong, I thought. There are too many opportunities for failure. Instead of listening to this overly cautious mind-set, I decided to take a rare step out of my comfort zone, and the results were life-changing.

Where before I felt personally and professionally confined by the difficulties of flying with a wheelchair, this trip to San Francisco opened up my world by showing me that air travel is a real, albeit difficult, option for me.

At the same time, it's absurd that I had to go to such lengths just to utilize a service that should easily be available to me. If fair and equal treatment under the ADA means sitting in a baby's car seat with a belt strapped around my waist and three trained caregivers maneuvering and situating me, maybe it's time to reevaluate what fair and equal means. Not to mention, I'm extremely privileged to have the financial resources and support network needed to pull off such an involved trip.

If you or someone you know has any sort of connection to the people who make these regulations, I'm asking you with sincerity to further explore allowing spaces for electric wheelchair users in the cabins of commercial airlines. I promise we won't bite the other guests.

Chapter 15

Hannah and Shane Take Manhattan

My head was tipped back and my mouth was stretched open as wide as my atrophied jaw muscles allowed. Hannah was vigorously digging in the back of my mouth with her index finger. There was a chunk of onion stuck in my teeth from the meal we had just eaten at a diner in Bethlehem. She was helping me dislodge it.

This moment, I realized, was a perfect image of our relationship: absurdity, but enjoying every minute of it.

"I don't think I can reach it. Am I moving it?" she asked, laughing.

I tried to answer but her finger kept me from being able to form coherent words. I gagged as she grazed my uvula.

She removed her finger from my mouth. "What if I tried to use a straw?"

"You could. It's really not a big deal. I can just tongue at it while we drive." As usual, I didn't want to be a burden, but

Hannah was always attempting to assuage my lifelong worry with love and patience.

She ignored me and retrieved a long purple straw from my book bag. With gentle precision, she prodded at the piece of onion stuck in the far left corner of my mouth, like a dentist on the hunt for cavities.

She was smiling. She was beautiful.

Almost immediately, she pried the onion loose and my world was returned to rightness and normalcy. I thanked her, and we laughed about it as we pulled out of the diner parking lot, not caring if the customers inside had just witnessed our unusual excavation process.

Hannah and I were going on vacation. It was early September, and the chill in the morning air—floating in the open windows as we made our way out of town—carried with it the sad feeling of our looming separation. Hannah attended college in Minnesota. We'd been dating about four months, but we already both felt that something truly special was growing between us, and that meant making the most of our precious visits. We only had a few days together before she was flying back home for what might be several months apart.

In previous relationships, teaching my girlfriend how to care for me was always a careful, gradual process. With Hannah—due partially to the lack of time together, but more because she possessed a uniquely easygoing quality that helped me open up to her—the teaching was much quicker. During her first visit, barely two months after we met online, we had the idea to create a bingo board with all the more involved "caregiving tasks" that she needed to learn. In this way, we made a game out of showering me, brushing my teeth, and other such activities. From the very beginning, she made me feel like we'd been together for years, and that sort of trust is a rare feeling.

I'm a firm believer that you can only truly know someone by experiencing adversity with them, and if that's true, we had plenty of opportunities early on to know each other.

For instance, a few months before we ate together at the diner, on her second visit, we took a day trip to New York City. The night before the trip, my wheelchair of over ten years took its final breath and turned off for the last time. It was a devastating moment. When I was done weeping and cursing the heavens, Hannah and I discussed whether we could still take our big trip. Luckily, I had my backup wheelchair waiting in the garage (which was technically my brand-new chair, but for a variety of stupid reasons, I never made the switch). However, this backup chair had numerous seating and comfort issues, and I wasn't confident in my ability to traverse the bumpy New York City landscape in a chair that basically didn't fit me. If that sounds like me being a spoiled diva, imagine you were told you needed to hike through a rocky jungle in eight-inch high heels for ten hours. You would not be enthused.

Over the next few hours—from 9 p.m. to midnight—Hannah and my parents worked together to help me retrofit the chair with supports, straps, and cushions that would allow us to continue with our scheduled plans. As I fell asleep that night, I was filled with conflicting emotions—gratitude for my parents and girlfriend for working so tirelessly to ensure my comfort, and fear that even with all the modifications, my body was too weak to make it through our trip the next day.

Morning arrived quickly. Our bus for the city left at 6 a.m., so when the alarm sounded at 5 a.m., we'd only gotten about four hours of sleep. Hannah got me dressed and out of bed in the soft early light. It was going to be perhaps the hottest day in recorded human history, a sweltering one thousand degrees, with enough humidity to turn my balls into a swampy steam bath before we'd even left my bedroom. Perfect conditions for an already stressful day.

We made it to the bus depot and got on the correct bus with minimal difficulty, despite the bus driver's apparent surprise at the fact that his bus even had a wheelchair lift. The new chair was annoying—for instance, I was already struggling to keep my arm in the proper driving position—but it was working, and my attitude shifted from nervousness to excitement about our first big adventure together.

Both of us dozed on the bus during the two-hour drive to New York. At some point, a pothole on the highway jostled me awake. Hannah was curled up in her seat next to me. I felt like the luckiest man alive.

We got off the bus at Port Authority, enjoying the stench

of human pee for twenty-five minutes while the driver once again acted surprised that there was a person in a wheelchair on his bus. Had it not been for Hannah showing him how to operate the lift, I might've been stuck on the bus forever.

Our first objective was finding food. I stupidly hadn't used my feeding tube the night before, which meant my body was functioning on severely depleted resources. The risk of my blood sugar dropping is much higher after skipping my tube, and that would be a catastrophe to deal with in the middle of New York City.

We walked ten blocks in the suffocating humidity—ninety-six degrees by 9:30 a.m.—and came across a Mexican-looking diner that served only American food. The inside was cramped, making it hard to maneuver my wheelchair to a table, but I smashed my way through and we ordered. As we ate, I noticed that my wheelchair battery was already at 9/10 bars. Slightly disturbing, but my corned beef hash was a more pressing matter at that moment.

A stranger came to our table and told us that Jesus loved us. He left us a $20 bill to pay for our meal.

Our next destination was Central Park, mostly because we wanted to relax in the shade while planning out our day. Unfortunately, on the twenty-block walk, my chair battery dropped to 8/10 and then 7/10 bars. My old chair could go a week on a single charge, so I had not at all been expecting my new chair to have issues with a single day. If there was any solace to be found, it was that I had my chair charger in my book bag. Granted, it takes eight hours to charge my chair, but I had the comfort of knowing I wasn't completely shit out of luck.

Did I mention that I was sick? That's probably an appropriate detail to add here. So not only was I using a new wheelchair that didn't fit me, with a battery that was failing, and an exhausted body from skipping my tube, but I also had a cold that resulted in multiple bouts of mucus hacking as we navigated the frantic streets.

In the park, we rested beneath a tree, both of us soaking with perspiration. I could barely breathe due to a chunk of phlegm lodged in my right lung. My chair battery was at 5/10 bars. All we could do was laugh as we poured water on our heads and figured out how we were going to charge my chair in New York City.

The rest of the day was grueling—and by far one of the best days of my life. Let me take you through some of the highlights, and I even have pictures to go along with them:

We made it to the Museum of Natural History with 2/10 bars of battery. I can count on one hand the number of times my battery has been that low in my life. Something was clearly wrong with this battery. Our plan was to tour the museum for a few hours in order to escape the punishing heat outside, a plan that was apparently shared by all thirty-two million people in New York that day. The museum was overrun with sweaty people. It didn't matter, though; as soon as we entered, my chair began to die, and I was forced to charge it at the only

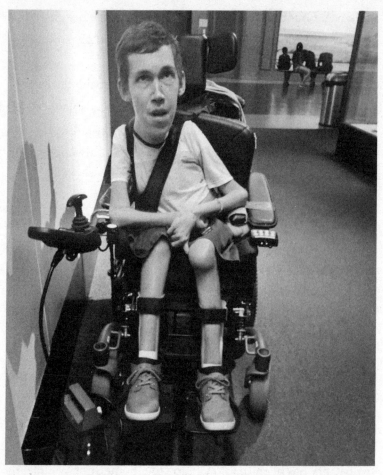

Charging my wheelchair in a random hallway in the Museum of Natural History, as millions of visitors stream past, giving me concerned looks.

outlet in the whole damn building, right in between two exhibits.

Hannah sat on the floor next to me while my chair charged, joking about how vagrant we must look. It became obvious pretty quickly that today was not going to be what we had imagined. Our discussion shifted from what activities we'd do, to where we could find another outlet. Coffee shops felt promising, so we agreed to find lunch and then a coffee shop for further charging.

Meanwhile, my burden complex was having itself a field day in my head. I was single-handedly ruining our first adventure together because of my wheelchair. This was it. She'd realize how annoying it was to date me, and it would all come crashing down. I must have expressed this as we walked the few blocks to Shake Shack for lunch because I have a vivid memory of Hannah stopping me in the middle of the sidewalk. She sat down on a stoop next to me and took my hand in hers. Our fingers fit together so naturally, and the drips of sweat served as lubrication for an even easier interlocking.

"Shane, stop. There's nothing in the world I'd rather be doing right now. This is hilarious, and we're having an adventure!"

Her smile calmed me, and I knew, as we leaned in for a steamy, romantic smooch, that she was being honest. It was true; as frustrating as it was, the day was less than half over and we already had a beautiful memory together.

My chair was dying fast, less than ten minutes after leaving the museum, so I waited on the sidewalk while Hannah ran into Shake Shack for takeout.

We made it to a little coffee shop a few blocks away where we sat for two more hours of charging. To keep ourselves entertained, we played a game where we pretended to be on a blind date gone horribly wrong. As the day progressed into late afternoon, I contemplated our journey back to Port Authority. We had about forty blocks to walk, which seemed doable by the time the last bus left at 10:30 p.m. We'd get dinner, then take our time wandering back. At least, that was the plan.

My wheelchair had other ideas in mind. By the time we arrived at a cozy Irish restaurant an hour later, my battery was almost completely empty again. I was about ready to ditch the stupid chair and ask Hannah to carry me the rest of the way. My body was also growing weary by this point in the day, a result of the heat, my illness, the new wheelchair, and miles of driving across the bumpy terrain of New York City. It was getting dark, and I wanted to leave plenty of time to make it back to the bus station in case we had to charge my chair along the way. Still, in the midst of such frustration and physical distress, all I felt was thankfulness for Hannah and for the life I was living.

I'm sure you have guessed by now that we didn't make it back to the bus. We made a valiant effort, hightailing it on Seventh Avenue as the clock (and my battery) ticked down. For the last couple of blocks, Hannah cradled my neck as we walked since I was no longer able to hold my head up. I was utterly spent and nearing hysteria as, on Sixtieth Street, my chair once again began to die—with still twenty blocks to go. We had no choice but to enter a nearby mall, where we begged the cashier in a fancy lotion store to let me charge my chair behind the counter. She allowed it, and the picture we took there may be the best representation of our day. I bought lime-flavored lip balm as a thank-you.

God bless L'Occitane.

Back out into the city streets! I made it a whopping five more blocks before the battery died again. Thankfully, we were near a Starbucks, which we entered like soldiers returning from a merciless war.

We decided (or accepted) that we were not going to make it back to the bus station in time. My parents were currently on a vacation of their own, in Maine, so they wouldn't be able to come pick us up, and I didn't think it was appropriate to ask a friend to drive two hours to rescue us in the middle of the night. We searched for nearby hotels and found one that had rooms available. At last, relief was in sight!

I'll never forget the feeling of getting into bed with Hannah that night, collapsing into each other in pure exhaustion,

Zonked.

with slimy skin and matted hair, a pile of our wet clothing growing moldy on the floor below (clothing we would have to put back on in the morning). It was surely a disturbing sight to behold, but we didn't care. We fell asleep instantly, without blankets, fan on high, and a deep comfort that only could have come from traversing such great adversity together. And we even remembered to plug my wheelchair into its charger.

Chapter 16

Adaptation

It was my dad's fifty-fifth birthday, and a good chunk of my family was crammed into my newly renovated basement man-cave/writing room/bedroom/sex dungeon. I quieted everyone for a special demonstration.

"Ladies and gentlemen," I said, "thank you all for coming today. I know you're ostensibly here for Dad's birthday, but it's obvious that the real reason you came was to see my new room."

Half of them groaned. Andrew told me to shut up. A few of my grandparents didn't understand what was going on.

"Please allow me to blow your minds." I cleared my throat. "Alexa, play some salsa music!"

A small cylindrical device lit up neon blue in the corner of the room. This was Alexa, a new product from Amazon designed to completely automate your home—from music to weather to shopping lists to calendars. She changed my life (we'll get to that), but back then, she was still having some trouble learning my voice.

Alexa spoke in her seductive electronic voice, but unfortunately, she misunderstood my request for music, responding, "You have seven items on your shopping list."

Oh God. This was bad. Everyone was listening intently, but it was too late to stop her. I wracked my brain, trying to remember what joke items my brother had added last night when we were testing out the new device.

"Milk, extra-small condoms, Vagisil for my vagina, Shane sucks, apples, more Vagisil, butthole butthole butthole."

Andrew was in hysterics on the couch. My mom looked at me like I had murdered one of her cats. I said, "Alrighty! Welp, that's enough of that! How about we all head back upstairs and celebrate Dad's birthday!" I could hear my grandfather muttering something about inappropriate language as they filed out of the room.

Adaptive technology—devices and technology that help people accomplish activities made challenging by their disabilities—is not always perfect, but if you set aside tiny mishaps like this, it has truly revolutionized my life and given me incredible independence. The fact is unavoidable: The environment and our society are not constructed with disability in mind, which is why we, meaning people with disabilities, have become experts in adaptation. In nature, species adapt to the environmental challenges that they face in order to thrive. When lizards realized—holy shit!—there's way more food *under*ground, they adapted by making their legs fall off and becoming snakes that could slither into tiny holes in the Earth. Can you tell I'm not a scientist?

Evolutionary changes such as these obviously take place over millions of years, but it still shows how organisms will do whatever it takes to survive in their environment.

A few years ago, as my disease began dealing heavier blows to the strength in my wrists and fingers, I learned how crucial adaptation was in my life. One of my favorite activities was playing the soccer video game *FIFA*. Sports have always been a huge part of my life, and while I was able to sort of half-play them in my wheelchair, nothing got me closer to the action than sports-simulation video games. With a game like *FIFA*, I was right there on the pitch, controlling every aspect of my players' movements. When I had friends over to play *FIFA*, you could hear us screaming at the TV from a block away.

Unfortunately, a game like *FIFA* required a high level of finger dexterity. In order to make your player sprint and turn and pass and defend and shoot, many buttons and levers needed to be pushed and pulled all at once. As my disease progressed, I began losing the ability to play my favorite game. I started to lose every match I played. It really blew. For a while, my friends enjoyed their newfound success, but eventually it became apparent that their wins were not a result of their skills but of my hands going to shit.

One afternoon, my best friend Pat and I were lazing around the house. He asked if I wanted to play *FIFA*, and I uncharacteristically declined.

"Oh, that's right, you suck now," he said. We started talking about the new issues I was having with my hands and how it appeared that our *FIFA* days were coming to an end. But then Pat had an idea: "Could we build some kind of contraption to help you push the buttons?" It sounded like one of those ideas that seems plausible in theory, but requires too much effort and skill to ever come to fruition. Pat, however, was already standing and making his way to the basement.

He returned with a hot glue gun and an assortment of random supplies: pencils, paper clips, wood, an eraser. We began tinkering and toying with different solutions. There was really only one button on the controller (R2) that I had fully lost the strength to press. We decided we might be able to fashion an attachment that would allow me to use a different finger to access this button.

We chopped up pencils. We bent paperclips, knifed rubber, melted plastic, and more. After almost two hours of work, just as we used up the last of my mother's hot glue (sorry Mom), our masterpiece was complete! It wasn't pretty, in fact it was an abomination, but it worked! With the slightest flick of my thumb, I could now press the required button again. We went in my room to test it and I kicked Pat's ass harder than I had in months (I don't actually remember if I won, but it's my book, so if I say it, it's true. You suck, Pat).

With a progressive disease like spinal muscular atrophy, it can often feel like life is a giant downward slope, like you're constantly moving backward on the ability scale. For every achievement or success, there always seems to be two more steps backward. I'm painting with broad strokes here, but you get the idea. This is why adaptation is so vitally important to me. Whether I'm using actual adaptive equipment, like the specialized seat I need to sit on the toilet, or hackjobs like my modified video game controller, I am able to reverse the downward trend of my disease, maintaining function that I would lose otherwise.

I often speak about the need to "make it work." It's such a simple idea, but I find it to be incredibly profound. Like the reptiles that abandoned their legs in search of food, I've developed a variety of adaptations that help me live happily and comfortably.

At night, once I'm arranged in my sleeping position, I can't move unless I call someone to roll me. In my teens, I began getting sores on my ears because they were smushed against the pillow all night. So, we took a memory foam pillow and cut a hole in it. Boom. Ear pillow. Comfort.

Also, before I go to sleep at night, I—like everyone else my age—enjoy being on my phone to text or play games or read. I can't hold my phone while lying in bed, so in high school, I purchased a twenty-dollar extendable arm that clips to the side of my bed and holds my phone in a reachable position. Boom. Phone holder. Function.

I can't itch my face, so I keep a straw nearby to scratch it. Boom.

I've lost the ability to chew food, so I use a feeding tube at night. Boom. How annoying are these booms?

Sometimes my head falls over in the car, so we turned a neck brace into a head-holder-upper. BOOOM.

Most recently, I wanted a way to control the music and lights and heat in my remodeled basement, and the Amazon Alexa device provided a perfect (most of the time) solution. When it's not making my grandparents think I'm a psychopath, the device gives me the independence to control my

Horribly ill-advised cup holder. BOOM.

environment. As I continue to lose more strength, I will need to adapt further. But that's the most beautiful part about "making it work." Despite the fear and uncertainty of my condition getting worse in my future, I can live with relaxed confidence, knowing there will always be a way to overcome the next hurdle that life throws at me. I can't reverse the disease, but adaptation makes the downward slope less steep.

Chapter 17

Your Complete Guide to Shane's Sex Life

Society has a disturbing infatuation with my sex life, and I'm not saying that in a Donald Trump "Everyone is so obsessed with me!" kind of way.

My blog has always had a feature that allows readers to anonymously ask me anything they want to know, and by far the most common questions are about my bedroom business affairs and the functions of my reproductive system.

Initially, it tickled me to respond to these questions publicly, because everyone seemed so impressed that "someone like me" could and did engage in sexual activity. I felt special, like a rare breed of the disabled population who had overcome the social stigmas surrounding disability to such an exceptional degree that I was worthy of sex. This, I later realized, was completely inaccurate, immature, and idiotic.

Sex and intimacy for people with physical disabilities is just as common and diverse as it is for any subpopulation of people. My desire to see myself as special or better than others in that sense was nothing more than a childish effort to bolster my insecurity-ridden ego.

Nonetheless, the general public's deep curiosity about my sexual abilities suggests there is an overwhelming lack of understanding regarding this issue. In an effort to clear up some of the confusion, here are a smattering of questions I've been asked by real people, as well as responses that I'm refreshing for the purposes of this book. Keep in mind, my experiences, shortcomings, methods, abilities, and inabilities are not meant to be representative of the disability community, the wheelchair-user community, or even the SMA community.

And now that I've belabored the point long enough to guarantee I won't receive angry reviews for this chapter, I will begin.

People have asked me:

"Do you have a penis?"

Yes, six of them, actually. Every time one of my major muscle groups begins to weaken because of my disease, I grow an additional penis. It's an interesting—albeit rather useless— perk of spinal muscular atrophy.

"Can you get a boner?"

I can! They've been coming in heavy and healthy ever since puberty hit, and I guess even earlier than that, but prior to puberty I had no idea what they meant. When I was

Zero working legs but half a dozen working dicks.

a little kid, I used to get them while lying facedown during physical therapy because of the way my groin pressed against the floor. That always made for an awkward surprise when the therapist rolled me onto my back for a new stretch. And that's a detail I've never shared with anyone until I wrote this book!

From what I understand, even though the penis contains muscles, the act of a boner rising to attention is more about blood rushing to that area of the body than muscle strength. My disease does not affect my blood flow.

"Do you masturbate?"

I wish I had kept a count of how many people have asked me this question through my blog. People question me about this so often that it's baffling. I try to imagine someone reading my blog—stories about breaking my femur, getting pneumonia, fearing death, going to the beach, etc.—and after all that information, the one thing they just need to know about me is if I fondle my own penis. Not that our lives are remotely comparable, but this feels akin to reading a biography on Abraham Lincoln and coming away from the experience wondering only if he became constipated very often throughout his lifetime.

For all you perverts, I had the ability to masturbate until I was about eighteen years old. The trickier part of the whole process was the cleanup, which involved pretending my nose was running so that someone would give me a bunch of tissues. Throughout my teen years, I was plagued with a constantly running nose, or so it seemed.

When my arms and hands became too weak to continue this activity, my dignity took a hit. It felt like I was losing part of what made me a valuable man. I took solace in the fact that my penis worked, and that in the grand scheme of things, being able to jizz in a clump of tissues wasn't the most important ability.

"Can you/do you have sex?"

I can and I do, although my physical structure and ability require some adaptation in the process. First, since I know my grandparents are reading this, I'll explain how my disease complicates standard, basic, run-of-the-mill sex, and then I'll share why I believe my disability actually improves sex and intimacy for my girlfriend and me.

As I've already established, my dick itself works phenomenally. The complications, then, are related to my muscle contractures. My body is stuck in a pretty rigid shape. When you don't use your muscles, they shrink, and eventually they become permanently tight. When I lie on my back, my body remains frozen in the sitting position, like a capital L tipped on its side. To imagine this, lie on your back and pull your heels up until they touch your butt. Perfect, now you're me!

The fact of the matter is that having sex requires certain parts of the body to be very close to each other, and when one of the participants is a crumpled mess of atrophied rigidness, that closeness can be tough to achieve. My partner can't simply hop on top of me, because if she did, my legs would smash into smithereens, and I suspect that would take some of the pleasure out of the experience.

Making love, then, becomes about finding positions that work. This often involves lots of bending, twisting, and contorting, which is why I only date gymnasts. My girlfriend and I have found some methods that work for us, and while we might look like a pair of grappling spiders, all that matters is that we're both enjoying the experience.

Early on it tortured me that I couldn't be a "better" sexual partner. My head was filled with damaging ideas about the importance of a man being able to perform in bed, and at times in my life, I was convinced that no woman in her right mind would ever want to be intimate with me. But as I became older and more experienced, I began to realize that intimacy in a relationship is so much more about the emotional connection than the physical one. SMA actually strengthens that aspect of my relationship. Having fun together physically requires us to communicate and listen to each other, which in turn makes us both much more aware of the other's pleasure. We've discovered that using our hands and mouths (and toes) is just as much fun as The Sacred Act. Once I abandoned the idea that sex needs to conform to society's narrow and ignorant guidelines—man dazzles woman by how hard and strong and fast he can gyrate his hips into hers—my sex life became much healthier and more enjoyable.

"Can you have children? Will they inherit your disease?"

Spinal muscular atrophy is a genetically transmitted disease, so there is a chance that any Shane Juniors I create will have the disease, but the likelihood of that happening depends on whether or not the mother of my kids is herself a "carrier" of the disease. One in forty people carries the genetic mutation that causes SMA. My parents, although they don't have the disease, are each carriers, which meant there was a one in four chance their kids would get it. It gets real science-y if you want to know more about it than that.

My plan is to have enough children with SMA so that our family outings look like some sort of day program for people with disabilities.

Chapter 18

Another Bathroom Story

You can't truly know that you want to spend forever with someone until you've pooped in their arms.

Hannah and I were spending the weekend at a friend's house in Connecticut. One night, after a wonderful evening of food and drinks with her friends, we retired to our guest bedroom. It was late and we were exhausted, so when Hannah asked me about showering or using the bathroom, I declined. The memory foam mattress was calling my name.

Three hours later, I awoke in the confusing, hazy dream-state that accompanies waking up in a strange location. I gathered my bearings and felt a vague discomfort in the pit of my stomach. As always, Hannah had somehow managed to steal all seventeen blankets that we had previously been sharing. Despite being exposed to the elements, I found that I was drenched in a thick layer of sweat. My stomach gurgled.

"Hey, babe? Can you roll me?" I whispered, knowing

it would probably take a few tries to rouse her from her slumber.

She murmured incoherent gibberish, and reached over to adjust my ankle by a few inches.

"Nope! Almost!" I tried again. "Hannah? Can you wake up to roll me, baby?"

She snuggled closer to me and whispered, "I'm just looking for the vein."

"Hannah, can you please wake up? I think something might be wrong."

The panic in my voice snapped her out of the sleep trance. She popped up onto her elbow, immediately awake, and asked what I needed. The discomfort in my stomach was gaining strength, and it felt like every inch of my body was dripping with sweat. I was shivering, and there was an elephant sitting on my chest, making it difficult to breathe.

I very rarely have stomach issues, and the few times throughout my life when I have had them, they usually evaporated pretty quickly. My muscles don't work, but I have the intestinal fortitude of an ox.

I suggested that I should try to pee—my 3 a.m. logic telling me that urinating might somehow solve the problem. Hannah began to climb out of bed to find my pee jar, but her movement sent a wave of nausea tearing through my body. I swallowed several times to avoid puking on our friend's mattress.

"Oh God, hold on. I need you to stop moving," I said. My

tone must have been urgent, because Hannah froze mid-movement. Minutes passed with agonizing slowness, as I focused all of my mental and physical energy on not throwing up.

When the contents of my stomach realized that the northern passageway had been sealed off, they made an about-face and set off toward the southern exit with gusto. Their journey was not a quiet one. The army trudged along, beating their drums, thrusting their torches into every inner crevice, stabbing my organs with their pitchforks, and bellowing their haunting war cries.

The outward manifestation of this violent internal siege laid upon my bowels was just a soft, repeated moan escaping from my lips. It probably seemed like I was being actively possessed by a demon.

"I think I'm going to have diarrhea," I whimpered.

Hannah sprang into action, snatching my specialized toilet seat from our suitcase and moving toward the bathroom to set it up in the dark.

Sensing that the army was approaching its target, I called to her, "I'm going to need you to hurry." This sent me into another series of convulsions. Someone had their fists wrapped around my stomach and was squeezing tighter and tighter.

I closed my eyes and slipped back into the fever dream.

Seconds later, I awoke again and found myself cradled in Hannah's arms, being carried toward the bathroom. The ten-foot walk seemed to take hours, as I concentrated every ounce of my determination on avoiding eruption in the hallway. I remember looking up at Hannah's face and feeling the comfort of her sleepy smile wash over me like warm water. I was dating an actual goddess.

Here I was in the midst of a full-on catastrophe, ravaged by what was about to be an atomic finale. I was cold and sweating and scared and naked and vulnerable, and yet, I felt no semblance of the embarrassment that you might expect. In fact, as she lowered me onto the toilet, and the guttural splashes filled the room with sounds and smells, she began to laugh and rub my back while keeping me steady atop the toilet.

Love is a difficult feeling to describe, but I can assure you it feels something like that moment, when the whole crazy mess of it reduced me to shaking laughter in her arms.

Chapter 19

Coughing

Each time, it begins with the slightest tickle in the throat, a tiny scratching that should easily be washed away with a sip of water, or at least that's how it seems.

When water doesn't do the trick, I know that a coughing fit is on the way, because it's not just a simple scratchy throat, but an irritation in my airway, a small but dangerous nugget of phlegm starting to form in my windpipe. I hunker down and prepare for the impending storm.

It's important that I don't cough too early. There will be plenty of time for that. Right now, energy consumption is key. I place my fork on the table, stop eating, and focus my attention on taking slow, deep breaths. My eyes begin to water as I resist the cough that's building in my chest. The length of my resistance is dependent on the environment I'm in. If I'm in public, I fight off the urge to cough as long as possible—what's about to ensue will be noisy and embarrassing—but if I'm alone, I don't wait as long to begin.

The first few coughs always escape unintentionally, literally forcing their way out of my lungs. They're usually weak and pathetic, quick hiccups of air, like a sputtering engine coming to life. Once they're out, there's no holding back.

I have no choice but to embrace it. There's no phlegm yet, but I promise you it'll be here soon. For now, my dry coughs simply amplify the scratching in my throat. The coughing increases, and this is the part where people around me typically notice that something is going on.

"You okay?"

"Need a sip of water?"

I'm grateful that my friends and family are so attentive to my breathing. I shake my head yes for okay and no for the water. If I could get words out between the rapid jags, I'd say that while it may *look* like I'm drowning, I'm in perfect control. Stressed, yes. Scared, yes. But still in control. I've learned the progression of my coughing fits, and I know the time and focus it takes to get through them.

The phlegm begins to build—tiny crackles felt deep in the cavernous pockets of my lower right lung. Long ago, I was told by a doctor that I would probably always have phlegm in this area, a result of the twisted shape of my rib cage. Most of the time it lies dormant, but each coughing fit brings the phlegm roaring back to life, gurgling its way up, searching for an exit. Each successive cough makes the rumbling grow louder, and it now feels like there's a pocket of bubbling liquid in my chest. The coughing is no longer involuntary. The itch in my throat is gone, but I now must work to clear the phlegm that's stirred up. I cough with as much force as I can muster, taking deep breaths between each burst to give myself the best chance of expelling some phlegm. My chest is extremely weakened by my disease, so after a few good coughs, I need to rest. During the rest, my breathing is labored. It's harder to get enough oxygen when you've got a lungful of nastiness working itself into a frenzy.

These fits can take anywhere from ten minutes to several hours. When the phlegm gets too serious, I have several machines that I can use to assist me with coughing. I'm never really in danger, but it's a fatiguing process, and one that reminds me of my always-decreasing lung function.

As I get older, these obnoxious coughing fits happen more frequently, and it seems to take less to initiate them. For instance, last week I made the dire mistake of laughing too aggressively with a mouthful of rice. One of the kernels (is a piece of rice called a kernel?) shot into my airway for a split second before I coughed it out, but a lengthy phlegm festival was triggered in the process. My own spit seems to seep into my airway and set off a cough-a-thon at least several times a week. Like all aspects of this disease, the changes are slow and tough to measure unless viewed from the perspective of five or ten years, but coughing has become a part of my daily routine, and that makes me worry about what my lung function will be like in the future.

Why am I sharing this with you? Well, for starters, yesterday I had the most delicious spaghetti experience interrupted by one of these obnoxious coughing fits. But more so because as I write this, winter is coming, and for someone living with spinal muscular atrophy, that means the looming threat of illness. Each year I wonder how my lungs will hold up if I happen to catch a cold. This is the cheerful thought I contemplate while I sip my pumpkin spice latte and watch the leaves fall from the trees.

But my thoughts aren't all bleak. I see the coughing as a little reminder to live harder and with more passion than I did the day before. Life is precious and beautiful, and no amount of coughing is going to change that.

Chapter 20

If I Could Walk

In early 2016, I gave a talk at Clearview Elementary School to a classroom full of fifth graders. I was there with my dad, who is the author of an awesome children's book called *The Sidecar Kings*. We were visiting the class to discuss the book and share my real-life story of disability with the young readers. Speaking to kids is always an interesting experience because they usually speak their true minds regarding my disability. When talking to these young audiences, I always have to put on metaphorical armor to guard my emotions against their uncensored questions.

And trust me, I've gotten some crazy ones.

Why can't you pee on your own? What's wrong with you? Do you sleep in your wheelchair? Do you sleep? Why do you talk like that? Can you walk? Can you read? What if your house has steps?

These questions make me chuckle, because there's nothing

offensive about them. They come from an honest lack of knowledge. That's why I do these speeches: to help kids fill in the gaps in their knowledge about disability in their developing brains and to show them that I'm just like everybody else.

At my most recent talk, a little girl asked me a question that I've been asked a million times: "What is the first thing you would do if you could walk?"

Every time I get this question I give a quick, lame answer like, "I'd love to be able to skateboard." Kids love that response, because it's something they can identify with, something they can imagine. I watch their eyes light up with wonder as they picture me climbing out of my chair and hopping on a skateboard. Plus, it's an honest answer. I have yearned for the ability to skateboard many times throughout my life.

But after this talk, when I was lying in bed trying to fall asleep, I found myself giving careful thought to the question. Is skateboarding truly the first thing I would do if I were suddenly cured of my disease? Is it even possible to know a real answer to this extremely hypothetical question? My brain loves to dig up huge philosophical issues whenever I'm trying to sleep. Thank you, brain.

Would I run a marathon? Would I drive to the beach and go surfing? Would I jump on a trampoline? Climb a tree? Go swimming? Kick something? Try skydiving? Each new idea gave me a surge of pleasure, as I imagined myself being able to explore the world with zero limitations.

All of these activities are things I would love to try, but as

I lay there that night, alone in the dark without the ability to even roll myself over or turn my head, I realized something important about myself: The ability to walk would not affect my happiness.

When I was younger, this was not the case. I hated not being able to play sports and climb trees and ride bikes. To counteract this nasty feeling of inability, I developed adapted methods to involve myself in whatever my friends were doing, but there was always that wish that I didn't need to do things differently.

As I grew up, the activities I couldn't do shifted to things like driving a car, attending parties at houses that had steps, and staying out all night like my rebellious friends. Don't get me wrong; I wasn't plagued by constant sadness, but I did occasionally find myself thinking that life would be better if I could just stand up and walk.

But today, when I ask myself this hypothetical question—what's the first thing I'd do if I woke up tomorrow completely cured of SMA?—I have an entirely different answer.

I'd walk to my kitchen and make myself a cup of coffee. I love that jolt of caffeine into my bloodstream. It's good for the soul. Next, I would go outside and read a book in the early morning sunshine, sip my coffee, and listen to the world wake up around me. This has become a favorite activity of mine, and it helps my brain prepare for a day of work. The rest of my day would consist of doing nonprofit activities with my wonderful coworkers, eating delicious food, and jumping in the pool for a quick swim (only now I wouldn't immediately sink to the bottom of the pool!). In the evening, I'd make a fire outside with my friends.

That is what I would do first, if suddenly cured of my disease. No skydiving. No massive displays of physical ability. I'd just do all my everyday activities, because I really love my life.

We all go through stretches of time when life places us in undesirable situations. But I think it's cool that my desires have adapted over time to become more comfortable and satisfied with my disability.

I'm never going to be a professional skateboarder. That's a dream of the past, and it no longer upsets me. So from now on, when people ask me what I'd do with a miracle cure, my answer will be: I'll wake up and make myself a cup of coffee.

Because this is the life I know and love.

Chapter 21

Spinraza

I will most likely be dead before I turn 30. Even that estimate is a generous one. I have a disease called spinal muscular atrophy type II that has been slowly destroying all the muscles in my body for the last 18 years, 11 months, and 354 days. Eventually I will catch a cold, it will turn into pneumonia, and my body won't be able to fight it off, at least that's what all my doctors subliminally imply every time they tell me I'm lucky to have stayed out of the hospital for almost a year now. Look at that, you already know my deepest fear, the one that hits me like a train every single night when I'm trying to fall asleep; I don't know how much longer I have to live. We're practically dating.

—Excerpt from my very first blog post, June 1, 2011

As I reread my earliest blog posts (something I try to avoid because most of them make me cringe—how did I ever think "hella" was an adequate synonym for "very"?), I often wish I could go back in time and tell my younger self not to worry so much about dying. My writing serves as a kind of time machine, allowing me to peer into my past and observe how my mind handled the challenge of a wasting, weakening body and the ever-looming threat of death.

Most of the time, my solution was humor.

When I lost the ability to hold my head upright on the first day of school, I posted: "Trust me, life can throw you lots of shit, but if you can take a step back and laugh at your situation, everything becomes a lot easier to deal with."

When strangers stared at me in public, I reasoned it was because I looked like "an alien-like pterodactyl creature with a human head that uses a wheelchair."

When trying to understand why women seemed uninterested in me, I posted: "Oh, also the tiny fact that unless a miracle cure is found in the next few years, I'm going to eventually die, and that isn't a turn-on for most women."

When my jaw muscles began to weaken and affect my ability to talk, causing me to make a garbling fool of myself in front of my entire class, I posted, "Everything that had just unfolded was so completely awkward that it was hilarious."

My tendency to reframe all negativity in a funny way was not done without self-awareness. In one of my early posts, I wrote: "I've gotten really good at putting on fake smiles when everything is not okay, pretending I'm oblivious to the fact that my condition is constantly getting worse."

The world saw me as a happy-go-lucky funny guy who spouted rainbows of positivity, but inside my head, I was facing a nonstop loop of thoughts about death and decay. Fun, right?

In a way, I can place bookends on the early blogging days of my life and call those years the Gloomy Period. Don't get me wrong, I was having a blast—my blog exploding into the spotlight, a book deal, starting a company, documentaries, girlfriends!!!—but taken as a whole, much of my time between 2011 and 2014ish was spent fearing the physical demise that I fully expected to arrive at any moment. I spent many a night alone in my bedroom because everything just felt hopeless and grim. My humor in those days was probably a necessary distraction as much as anything else.

As I grew up, my experiences began to provide mounting evidence that my fears of imminent death might be less warranted than they seemed. I met more and more adults living with my disease who were kicking ass in their forties, fifties, and sixties, who had families and careers and didn't bat an eyelash at the abilities their disease had taken away, but who thrived on whatever abilities they did possess. I was told by more than a few of them that it was time for me to drop the melodramatic sob story they saw on my blog.

At first, I felt attacked. How dare they question my deepest fears and vulnerabilities? But the more I thought about it, the more I realized they weren't aiming to assassinate my character; instead, they were trying to wake me up and free me of the shackles I was creating for myself by situating every happiness I experienced as "happiness despite my wretched circumstances." These people weren't suggesting I ignore the difficult realities of SMA, but rather showing me that my life need not be *defined* by that hardship.

Their urgings ultimately helped me embrace my disability, and my inner torment about the future transitioned into a kind of passionate refusal to be victimized by my disease. I went to a doctor's appointment in early 2015 and was informed that my breathing had gotten objectively worse since the previous year. About that experience, I posted:

> . . . after the initial jolt of discovery, this time, all I felt was a relaxed, calm acceptance. I turned and smiled at my girlfriend, who was with me at the appointment that day. She smiled back. Yup, I'm getting worse. It's a slow worsening, just like it always has been, but I'm living with more intensity than ever before. There's just no sense agonizing in the darkness of things you can't control.

My humor, in turn, was granted some freedom to explore new subjects that did not directly relate to my disease. I posted a 621-word essay about a stink bug watching me poop. I got a job for the local paper and penned columns about soccer, staying healthy, and spreading kindness. I even started writing fiction that had nothing to do with me, and holy shit, I loved it!

An enormous weight was lifted off my chest when I realized that my disease did not need to be the focal point of my every waking thought and action. It was possible, I was learning, to just be "Shane the writer" or "Shane the boyfriend" as opposed to "Shane the disabled writer" or "Shane the disabled boyfriend." I felt an abiding sense of peace with this discovery.

With this new perspective in my cognitive arsenal of defense against SMA woes, I was better equipped to deal with a difficult 2016. My lungs were getting weaker and making it hard to sleep, my arms were getting weaker and making it hard to drive my wheelchair, and my jaw was getting weaker and making it hard to eat even the softest of foods. All of these losses took their toll, and I had plenty of moments where my disease took center stage for days at a time. Hannah played a crucial role in helping me through those periods, nudging me to embrace change as it came: "Will it really be so miserable to be spoon-fed your favorite soups by *me* for the rest of your life?"

Even with her support, I spent the year on an emotional roller coaster—one day on top of the world, ready to publish a hundred books and travel the world no matter what my disease had in store for me, and the next, when I discovered the loss of some ability, hardly able to muster a joke. Such was the unsettled, complicated nature of my existence until everything changed on December 23, 2016.

It was a Friday night, and I had just returned to my home in Pennsylvania after spending a week in Minneapolis to meet

Hannah's family for the first time. I was physically exhausted after seventeen hours in the car, but emotionally glowing with the satisfaction of being so thoroughly in love.

I opened my email, and as I scanned my inbox there was a subject line that stopped me short: "FDA Approves First-Ever Treatment for Spinal Muscular Atrophy." I reread it three or four times as my brain struggled to make sense of those particular words in that particular order.

My heartbeat moved up into my throat as I opened the email and read its contents. In a matter of a few paragraphs, my worldview was flipped upside down and shaken violently. There was a drug called Spinraza, being studied by a company called Biogen, and what they had discovered, it seemed, was that injecting this drug into the spinal cords of people living with SMA could effectively stop the progression of their muscle-wasting. The FDA had reviewed Biogen's findings and confirmed the drug's effectiveness. The treatment would be commercially available within a few weeks.

My first thought: This isn't a treatment, this is a fucking cure!

Spinraza is basically fake DNA that tells the body to stop being stupid and start creating the correct proteins for muscle growth and maintenance. It stops the progression of muscle loss, and in many recipients, there was even some reversal of the loss, meaning people gained back strength and ability.

Describing for you the intensity of the shock and disbelief I felt in the minutes that followed reading that email would

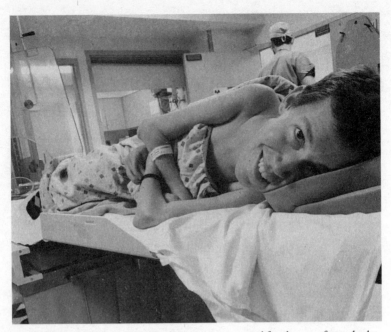

"We're about to jam a needle into the most precious and fragile part of your body. Smile!"

be a useless task. Words are comically inadequate for what I felt. Instead, I'll tell you what happened next.

My brother came into the kitchen. I said to him, with a voice that was fluctuating in an effort to remain steady, "So, they . . . apparently found a cure for SMA?"

He stopped. "What do you mean?"

Don't cry, Shane.

"Like, they've been studying this drug? And it apparently stops the disease?" I said.

Don't you dare cry, Shane Burcaw.

"Like, your muscles won't get any . . . worse?" he asked.

I nodded, but I happened to notice his wide eyes had the beginnings of tears forming in them and that sent me over the edge. My face opened its floodgates, and I cried the happiest, laughingest cry I've ever cried.

It wasn't long before Andrew broke the seriousness of the moment with a joke. "So then I don't have to help you pee tonight, right?"

The same basic scenario replayed itself several more times that evening as I told Hannah and members of my family. My brother ran to the store for champagne, and we celebrated well into the night with bright exuberance.

Several days later, after the initial excitement began to fade, I was left with a vague feeling of confusion about the drug. I wasn't as joyous as I thought I would (or should) be, but I couldn't put my finger on why. For so much of my life, the biggest obstacle to my freedom, my happiness, my safety, my well-being, my comfort, etc., has been my disease. As seen in my early blogging, my disability was such a big aspect of my identity that it started to become the defining aspect of my identity. Only recently had I started to transition away from that way of thinking.

But now, out of nowhere, there was a drug that promised to halt the progression of the disease and give me confidence in living an average life span without worry of getting worse. It would basically take away the scariest part of living with SMA—the decline. Even crazier, reports suggested that I could even gain back some previously lost strength. Wasn't that alone reason enough to wake up every morning and scream joy?

I was excited. But it seemed like everyone I told was significantly more excited than me. In fact, countless times in the months between reading the FDA announcement and getting my first injection, I found myself downplaying the significance of Spinraza in conversation, which often elicited disturbed expressions in response, as if I'd said I had won a billion dollars but wasn't taking the money. Ironically, I had recently published an article based on the "If I Could Walk" question. As you'll remember, the idea was that my life wouldn't change much, since I was already living pretty happily and successfully with my disease. Spinraza, to some extent, confirmed my arguments in that piece, and the arrival of a "cure" really didn't faze me. More than any other feeling, it made me uneasy.

It wasn't until I began receiving the injections almost a year later that I finally pinpointed why I felt so ambivalent about the drug. The potential to be "cured" of my disease had the unintended effect of causing everyone around me to see anything less than a complete cure as an unfortunate failure, which totally opposed the healthy embrace of my disease that I was working so hard to adopt.

Imagine a person was born with six legs. Having six legs made his life different, and at times, difficult—odd looks from strangers, clothing fit incorrectly, more toenails to cut—but, for the most part, he got used to having six legs and just wanted to go about his life normally. That's fair, right? It wasn't even very hard to do so, because the six-legged person was surrounded by friends, family, and acquaintances who supported this plan. Then one day, a brilliant scientist came along and said she had pioneered a method for removing extra legs! Everyone rejoiced, including the person with six legs. After all, living with six legs was annoying a lot of the time. Having two legs would be pretty sweet. But then, when it came time for the leg removal surgery, the surgeon realized she was only going to be able to remove one of the extra legs. The person who now had five legs figured this was still one less leg to lug around, so he was still thrilled with the surgery! Even if none of the legs had been removed, it didn't really matter, since life with six legs had been normal and even pretty great most days, like when he found cheap shoes or his girlfriend gave him a blow job. However, to his surprise, many of his friends and family and acquaintances seemed bummed that the surgery didn't work, asking him constantly if there was any possible way those extra legs could be removed someday. This made him wonder how genuinely everyone had supported his six-legged life before the surgery.

Spinraza was a drug that I'd be taking for the rest of my life, and its effectiveness varied from person to person. For instance, some people gained back arm strength after a single injection; others noticed increased stamina after a year of injections; many saw no increase in strength, but also saw no decrease, which is still a powerful outcome with a disease like SMA.

After my first two injections, I saw no difference in physical ability, and many people who received this information from me reacted with subtle sorrow.

"Don't give up, okay?"

"I've been praying for this for years. I believe it's going to work."

"When do you think it will kick in?"

At one point, even my dad couldn't help himself, using a flawed breathing test score to share happy news with our relatives. "It's finally working!" he wrote to everyone, despite the two of us having concluded that the test had been done incorrectly and that I felt no actual difference in lung strength. The texts of celebration that started to pour in after his family-wide announcement were tough to read without getting angry.

I get it. Everyone was excited for me and wanted the absolute best outcome, but when their ideal "best outcome" basically meant "not having SMA," it made me wonder if all these people, my closest friends and family, harbored negative attitudes and assumptions about my life prior to Spinraza being invented.

From my point of view, I've been living with spinal muscular atrophy since the day I was born. I'm used to it. I'm comfortable with it. I can and will live an extraordinary life full of laughter and love and success, regardless of whatever amount of strength I have at my disposal. I'm happy for the treatment, but don't necessarily need a cure.

If Spinraza happens to mutate me into an ultra-strong behemoth, great, catch me at the gym, but nothing else is going to change.

Chapter 22

StankTour

In the summer of 2017, Hannah and I spent a month traveling around the United States together on a massive road trip that we later named the StankTour, referring to how little showering we did along the way. When we returned home in August and told people about our epic vacation, we received the same stupefied response time and time again: "Wait, so, it was just the two of you? Like, she did all of your care? No nurses? No medical staff?"

Hannah and I had been dating for just over a year when the road trip idea was born, and although that year was technically a "long-distance" relationship, we somehow managed to make a visit happen almost every month of that first year, so she was already thoroughly acquainted with how to keep me alive. In fact, during our first year, my physical care had become one of the strongest facets of our relationship.

Each time she returned to her home in Minnesota, I deeply

missed the comfort of being lifted into bed by her, of having her shower me and help me use the bathroom. At the same time, maybe even more intensely than me, Hannah lamented that she was not the one brushing my teeth and putting my socks on each morning. Life was better for both of us when she was the person helping with my daily living. Obviously, our desire to be together had much less to do with the actual caregiving and much more to do with the fact that we were best friends (and in love). We made each other laugh and think, and waking up next to her each morning always felt like the start of a brand new adventure.

Over Skype in the months leading up to the trip, we mapped out our route and fantasized about the new places we'd see together. Once, my nervous nature got the best of me and I asked her something like, "You're sure after an eight-hour drive you'll be okay with doing all my stuff too?"

Her eyes rolled so far into the back of her head that the internet connection almost zapped out. When she regained control of her facial features, she repeated a line I'd heard from her before: "I love doing that stuff, Shane. It's the exact opposite of a burden. I want to be the one doing it."

She had a keen way of laying my fears to rest with that sarcastic roll of her eyes.

So yes, it was just the two of us on this road trip, and no, we didn't worry whether Hannah could handle all my care. Instead, we worried about . . .

BETHLEHEM, PA—Do we have the milkshakes?

Months of preparation had us feeling like no stone had been unturned. We'd examined this trip from every angle, and even though a large portion of the details were purposely left up in the air to allow for spontaneity, we still departed from my house on the first morning confident that the most important factors had been adequately anticipated.

One of those factors was how I was going to maintain a healthy level of nutrient intake throughout the weeks on the road. In my typical daily life, I rely on a nasal feeding tube to deliver the majority of my calories—about 1,500 per day. When I'm traveling, it's often easier to forego the nightly feeding tube and just drink one of the high-calorie protein milkshakes that my doctor prescribes for me. For our trip, I decided to rely solely on these milkshakes, putting them pretty high on the list of "important things not to forget," along with my wheelchair, Pringles, and plenty of underwear.

Guess what we forgot?

Luckily, we were still close to home when we realized we needed to turn around.

LAGRANGE, IN—Where the hell do you get food after 7 p.m. in rural Indiana?

Wanting to escape the drab repetitiveness of major interstates, we decided to venture off the main highway in Indiana to navigate the forgotten back roads of corn country instead. Peaceful farmland dotted by the occasional three-block "town" became the norm. We argued about whether cow manure was a pleasing smell as we crested the low, rolling hills and the sun set softly before us.

Nearing the small town of Shipshewana, Indiana, where we had booked our first hotel, our stomachs began to growl. I searched the GPS for somewhere to eat. It was 7 p.m. on a Wednesday, and to my confusion, not a single place was open. Not *one* within thirty miles. I'm not sure how anyone can survive without the occasional 10 p.m. deep-fried McDonald's fix, but apparently the wholesome people of rural Indiana are all in bed by mid-afternoon.

We located a family-run grocery store in a town that may have been home to six people. It was closing in ten minutes, but they kindly let us grab a meal suitable for royalty—frozen TV dinners and lemonade.

Astonishingly, our room at the quaint little inn not only had a microwave to heat our food, but a whirlpool bathtub right in the middle of the bedroom. It screamed indecency. Maybe those innocent Indianans aren't so pure after all.

SHIPSHEWANA, IN—Are we weird?

I can't think of a much sexier occasion than lounging the night away in a hotel bathtub. We undressed and Hannah lowered me carefully into the tub, steaming with scalding water from the surprisingly powerful faucet. I shrieked as the burning water enveloped my body. Mmm, fuck, sexy.

Taking a bath together was something we had talked about doing but never attempted because of the physical challenges. Outside of the carefully constructed supports of my wheelchair, I cannot hold up my head or move my limbs, so a bathtub full of water might as well be the middle of the Atlantic Ocean for me. To avoid drowning, I wore my adaptive neck float that I use for swimming. The plan was to remove it once Hannah climbed in and got situated.

A rare Mangled Sea Anemone in its natural habitat.

"It's way too hot," I said, floating in the tub while she took off the rest of her clothing.

"Can I run more cold water for my biggest baby?" she replied.

"Nah, I'm sure it'll cool off. Hurry up, this neck float is cutting off blood flow to my brain."

The sex tub was decently sized, but not wide enough for our bodies to lounge side by side. Hannah slithered down in a series of precarious postures, sliding me on top of herself as she got comfortable in the water. I yelped about my fragile feet and fragile hips and fragile ribs. She giggled and assured me she was being careful. I yelped some more. We both laughed. We kissed. She slid down a little further, more frantic yelping from me, and then we were settled.

"Holy shit," I said. "This is perfect."

"Our neighbors probably think I'm abusing you over here. *'Watch my feet!'*" she mimicked, leaning over to kiss my neck.

Our bodies were tucked together beneath the water, my head resting against her shoulder now that my float had been removed. Her arms, wrapped around me, made sure I didn't slip below the surface. The position felt so natural and effortless that I stopped worrying about my feet. We closed our eyes and listened to the chirping of summer crickets outside our window.

All too soon, our relaxing moment was complicated by the growing discomfort of soaking in boiling water on a humid July evening.

"Okay, this is the most comfortable I've ever been, and I don't want to move, but my face is beginning to tingle as I imagine it might before a heat stroke," I said.

"I've been trying to figure out how I can reach my water bottle without submerging you," she said.

My face was sweating. Her chest was sweating. I could feel the blood in my veins thickening into sludge. The end was rapidly approaching unless we cooled off fast.

Delicately, as if handling an infant, Hannah hoisted me onto her lap and raised us both into a sitting position. She reached forward and turned the bathtub faucet onto full-blast cold, sending a chill radiating up through our feet. She cupped her palm and filled it with the frigid water, splashing it in my face. She brought her next palmful to my lips. In my fervor to cool down, I drank, and as the icy water trickled over my dry lips, hysteria overtook me.

"More! Now!" I said, but she was already chugging a mouthful for herself, and then another, and then another. We took turns like that, sucking beautiful handfuls of water from her palms, until the tub water turned cold and it was time for bed.

Falling asleep that night, we decided bathtubs would not be the ideal venue for future sexy times.

SHIPSHEWANA, IN—Is this ethical?

We never expected the first stop on our trip to provide so many memories, especially considering Shipshewana, Indiana, isn't exactly known for being a travel destination, but the next morning, before setting off for Chicago, we wanted to see the area.

Shipshewana is home to the nation's third-largest Amish community, and a quick Google search brought up a nearby Amish-run "animal park" that—bizarrely enough—touted its wheelchair accessibility as a major bonus to all they had to offer. There was no way we could move on without checking this place out.

Two hours later, we found ourselves parked inside a vast animal enclosure, stricken with fear as a variety of hungry beasts attempted to enter our van. An ornery water buffalo with horns the size of parking cones brushed his spikes along the length of my van. An ostrich stood outside my window and stared directly into my soul. Something that appeared to be a woolly mammoth tried to mount the rear of the van.

Turns out, goats are totally pro-wheelchair.

It was neat for about three minutes before it became disturbing. The animals were definitely not too enthused about having a line of minivans driving through their habitat every day. I need to brush up on my Amish law, but the whole setup felt like it shouldn't be allowed to exist. We left.

CHICAGO, IL—Is there a bathroom here?

After taking the obligatory tourist photos in front of the giant bean in downtown Chicago, we meandered through the chaotic city streets until we came upon a tavern that caught our eyes. Once we had been seated, I asked our waiter if there was a bathroom nearby. He calculated a route in his head, and replied, "Yes, follow me."

We moved through the dining room and turned into a tight hallway. He stopped at an elevator and instructed us to get on. The three of us barely fit, so when a fourth individual— a chef, it seemed—joined us on the next floor up, the mood became quite sexual. We exited on the fifth floor.

He gave us further instructions: "Now, you're going to follow this hallway down and make the third left. That door only opens if you really tug it. Once inside, another attendant will take you back down two floors on the freight elevator to the backside of the building. Cross the drawbridge and blow out four of the six candles lining the altar that lies beyond. A bookcase will open. Enter it. Ignore the children. Take a right, then a left, and you'll find yourself in a room full of key-shaped fairies, only one of which will fit the lock to the accessible bathroom at the far right corner of the adjacent room. Good luck."

Thankfully, I had already peed in my pants during the first half of his explanation, so there was no need to bother with all of that.

MINNEAPOLIS, MN—What are the softest foods?

Throughout our trip, and especially during the week we spent at Hannah's parents' house in Minneapolis, we made it our mission to seek out soft food that would be easy for my weakening jaw to handle. Time and time again, while deciding where to eat dinner, Hannah would bring up various menus on her phone and read aloud the items that sounded most friendly for my mouth muscles. I ordered soup almost every day, and as she fed me spoonfuls, we wondered what wild assumptions nearby strangers were making about our relationship. Occasionally, we'd exchange a brief kiss to complicate whatever they were inaccurately imagining about us. We didn't care if they stared, and I ate to my heart's content without getting tired every night.

MURDO, SD—Why in the world did we think a Super 8 in Murdo, South Dakota, was going to be a nice place to spend a night?

No explanation needed. There were actual cockroaches in our room, and the best breakfast option the next morning was expired donuts and soggy cheese from the gas station next door.

BADLANDS, SD—Why did I wear pants?

My whole life, I've struggled to find comfortable, stylish clothing that I can wear. Pants have been particularly hard to find ever since the baggy clothing of the 90s went out of style. In fact, since my teen years, I'd say one of my biggest struggles has been finding skinny jeans that I can wear. Rough life, right?

I'm small, like slightly-larger-than-a-well-fed-toddler small. And my legs are basically locked into the sitting position of my chair, so when all my friends began wearing skintight jeans back in high school, I had to sit on the sidelines and watch with envious eyes as that fad passed me by. It was just too tough to find a pair of jeans that looked skinny on my stick legs but weren't so tight that they snapped my brittle twig bones as someone yanked them on each morning.

For a while, I just settled for being uncomfortable. I had one pair of jeans that I deemed cool, and even though putting them on took four hours, and even though the waistband gave me actual bruises on my hips, and even though taking them off was like peeling the skin off a highly sensitive apple using only your fingertips, I wore them every day because they were my best option. After high school, I gave up on this desire to be trendy and returned to wearing whatever clothing was easiest.

Then, while in Minneapolis on this road trip, Hannah introduced me to a magical world called the Girls section at H&M, a place bursting with soft material and stretchy fabric. Just thinking about it makes my eyes moist with joy.

Here I met the oxymoron that is called the stretchy skinny jean. They're a real thing, and they are exactly what they sound like: soft, comfortable jeans that melt into my curves like warm butter but stretch like putty for easy on and off. Plus, there is a thing in this magical land called "high waisted," which solved my lifelong problem of having my pants slip off my rear end when I'm being lifted from my bed to my chair.

Obviously, I wanted to wear them every day of the road

Getting sun poisoning in the Badlands!

trip, even when it was 105 degrees in the desert of a state park that is the Badlands. I roasted like a disabled chestnut on an open fire. By the time we got to our hotel in Wyoming later that night, I was sitting in a puddle of my own sweat.

Can I blame this on Hannah? She is my caregiver, after all.

YELLOWSTONE NATIONAL PARK—Is that it?

Old Faithful was a letdown. I feel un-American for even saying it, but it's the honest truth. It was the opposite of thrill-

Shortly after this, Hannah was distracted for an hour by a family of wild mice.

ing. Don't get me wrong, Hannah and I greatly enjoyed the rest of Yellowstone, and if you are one of my wheelchair brethren reading this, the park has many accessible trails and pathways and breathtaking sites to see, but the most famous of geysers felt like a lame tourist trap.

DENVER, CO—What's the plan?

In Denver, marijuana is legal for recreational use, so Hannah and I decided to give it a whirl. (My mother just put the book down to send me a disapproving text message.)

I'll spare you the cringeworthy details of actually purchasing the THC-laced gummy bears from the pot shop and bring you to later that evening when, after ingesting what we both thought should have been enough to give us a high, we were feeling sadly disappointed that nothing was happening.

The golden rule for edible weed products is to give your body plenty of time to digest. A common mistake that first-timers make, we were told, was not giving the edibles enough time to work their magic. People don't feel instantly high, and think they've purchased a dud, so they take more, and then everything they've taken hits at once, which can be a pretty scary experience, we were told.

We broke the golden rule.

Despite ingesting enough weed to kill a small cow, I was miraculously unaffected, which must be some freak symptom of muscular dystrophy—a hulkish immunity to weed—but

Hannah was not so fortunate, and it turned our night in Denver into one that we—or at least *I*—will never forget.

It began about halfway through our dinner at an upscale bar in downtown Denver. I asked Hannah if she was feeling the edibles yet.

"I don't . . . think?" she contemplated. "But I can't feel my legs?"

"Seriously? Or are you just being dumb?" I asked.

A few seconds passed before her eyes found mine again. "What?"

"What, what?" I said. Her stare wandered across the room. "Hannah, can you really not feel your legs?"

She turned her glance back to me with a visible amount of effort. "I feel like I keep waking up, like everything you just said was a dream, but I'm awake now. What did you say? I don't like this."

Fuck. This was not a good sign. I'd never eaten edibles before, but I'd been around plenty of people who had, and I knew the classic signs of having eaten too many. It was only a matter of time now before the all-encompassing sluggishness pressed itself heavily upon her body and mind. She was about to become a zombie, a really stupid zombie, and we were at least a forty-five-minute walk from the hotel.

"Hey, why don't we try to finish up so we can head back to the hotel," I said, keeping my voice light and breezy, lest my worried tone scare her into a bad trip.

Her stare was blank, her eyes drooping already. She spoke

in a slow, quiet whimper: "Oh, I don't like this at all. I feel like I'm watching myself and I can't feel anything. I can see myself talking. Is this bad? What did you say before about my phone?"

"Your phone? I'm not sure, baby. Hey, let's eat up and head out, okay? Are you full?"

"I think if I just lay for a little . . ." And she began leaning over in the booth.

"Hannah, we can't sleep here. We need to go back to the hotel, okay? You're probably going to feel very, very sleepy, but that's totally normal. I need you to stay awake until we get back to our room, okay? Think we can do that?"

The waitress stopped at our table and I asked her to bring the check. Hannah was wearing an expression of pure panic as she lost further control of her faculties. She seemed on the verge of crying. "How long was she standing there? Did I have time to reply?"

"You did great. I just asked her to bring the check."

On the way out, Hannah needed to use the bathroom. I waited for her outside the door. When she came out a few minutes later she said, "I didn't wash my hands. I was afraid I would forget you."

"Okay, psycho. Let's try to walk back to the hotel."

Our journey was quite an adventure. Her heart was beating a thousand miles per hour, she reported, which I knew was a normal symptom of too many edibles, but which felt to her like an impending heart attack.

She was beyond panic; she didn't have the energy for panic.

Instead, she melted into a state of resigned terror, like walking through a living nightmare.

We took it one block at a time. Some blocks were better than others. Several times she insisted that she just needed to lie down for a few minutes, and it physically pained me that I couldn't let her. At one point, her reflection in a glass window scared her enough that we had to stop for me to explain reflections and remind her of our goal of getting back to the room. On another block, she became insatiably thirsty, but her water bottle had seemingly disappeared from my backpack. (It was there.)

We kept onward.

"What should I do with this?" she asked, holding her phone out toward me.

"That's your phone. You just need to hold it."

"It's too heavy."

My favorite memory was when a severely decrepit woman who had to be at least 106 years old staggered up to Hannah on the sidewalk and leaned into her face.

"May I talk to him?" asked the woman, gesturing at me. Hannah looked at me like legions of bloody demons were massacring thousands of innocent children before her eyes. She had zero ability to process what was happening, but it was scaring her. So when the woman proceeded to grab my arm and scream prayers of healing, all we could do was take off in a new direction, Hannah holding back tears and using my wheelchair as a walking aid.

"I don't like this. I don't like this," she repeated.

We made it back to our room, and I asked Hannah, "What's the plan?" We'd been practicing her answer the whole way home.

She nailed it: "Get your laptop set up for you before I get in bed."

She executed the plan perfectly before falling asleep for a solid sixteen hours, only waking once when I roused her from sleep to lift me into bed around midnight.

Our experimentation with edibles was a failure, but as I watched Hannah sleep that night, monitoring the consistent rise and fall of her chest, my concern for her well-being was intensely palpable. Constantly being on the receiving end of care, I was not accustomed to that feeling of "taking care" of someone. So many times I have worried that Hannah was being burdened by my care. When I vocalized those concerns, she always refuted my fears, telling me that her love for me largely overshadowed any feelings of "caring" for me. Not knowing what it felt like to be in her shoes, it was easy for me to dismiss those statements, writing them off as something that she had to say because we were dating and it would be cruel not to say it. However, on the night of Hannah's epic plunge into edible-induced hysteria, our roles were slightly reversed for a few hours, and it made me realize I'd do anything to keep her safe. Suddenly, it seemed so obvious to me what she had been telling me all along. When you love someone with your whole heart, there's nothing you won't do to keep them safe and comfortable. It's not a sacrifice and it's not a burden; it's a natural instinct.

The next morning, while packing up our suitcases for the next leg of the road trip—down to Texas, then Louisiana, Florida, Georgia, and back up to Pennsylvania—Hannah brought up a topic we'd discussed with dreamy eyes many times, but which now felt realistic in a brand-new way. While lifting me into my chair, she said, "We need to live together."

Chapter 23

The Move

Guess what? That's exactly what we did. I can
barely believe it as I type the words, but I'm writing the last
chapter of this book from Minneapolis, Minnesota, where
Hannah and I now live together in our own apartment. It's
mid-April and snowing heavily outside, contradicting Hannah's
perpetual insistence that the weather in Minnesota "is actually
quite nice." In a few hours, Hannah will return from a long day
of classes. There is chicken thawing on the kitchen counter for
the pasta we are cooking tonight, and we plan on watching a
few episodes of *Criminal Minds* before bed. It's all so adult I
could puke. As I watch the snowflakes dance down outside
our window, I'm feeling a deep sense of contentedness with
the completely unexpected and totally astounding transfor-
mation my life has undergone in the last few months.

Several weeks after our big road trip around the United
States, Hannah was back at school a million miles away in

Minnesota, and our daily life settled back into its normal routine. It was a weekday evening, and I was in my bedroom FaceTiming. Hannah sat at the desk in her dorm room with a towel wrapped around her head, drying her hair after a two-hour swim practice. We were looking at flights for a short weekend visit in about a month, and as exciting as that should have been, the mood was dull and infused with a layer of stress that came from so much time apart.

"Here's one with no layover, but you'd need to leave on Thursday. Could you do that?" I asked.

Hannah sighed and moved to her bed, propping the laptop on her thighs. "I have no idea, it depends what's going on in my classes that week, but I won't know until that week."

We decided to wait and see, which felt more like agreeing that a visit probably wasn't going to be feasible. Our moods declined further, and we basically just sat in sulking silence together for a while. Fun night! Eventually, Hannah got up to put on her sleeping clothes, and in an effort to lighten the pressing sadness, I initiated an exaggerated praise of her naked butt as I watched her change.

She was giggling and becoming more interested in the playful striptease that she was performing when suddenly my bedroom door swung open. My mom walked in, unaware of the illicit activity she was interrupting. I must have looked like I was trying to smash an escaping beetle the way I abruptly slammed my mousepad to hang up the FaceTime call before she saw anything. Thankfully, I don't think she did.

When I called Hannah back a few minutes later, her clothes were back on and the mood had once again plummeted into despair. The weeks and months of time apart stretched out before us like an endlessly bleak desert of loneliness.

I'm not sure what made it happen. Perhaps it was the heavy accumulation of so much longing, but in that darkest of moments, a tiny spark of hope ignited itself and refused to be extinguished.

"What if we moved in together?" Hannah asked.

I laughed half-heartedly. "I mean, yeah, someday, definitely. But you still have two more years of school, plus maybe law school after that." My unspoken point being this: You certainly can't move to Pennsylvania right now, and me moving there would require more time, energy, and logistical solutions than we can practically handle with you being in school.

Hannah disagreed. She believed that I could easily move to Minnesota and we could begin our life together, and not only would it be easy, but the ultimate effect would be positive and beneficial for both of us. I'll admit, at first the idea absolutely terrified me. What felt like hundreds of unanswerable questions clogged up my brain so that I didn't even know where to begin.

Who will take care of me while Hannah is at classes? Where will we live? Where will I get Spinraza? What happens if Hannah gets hurt or sick or is otherwise unable to tend to me on any given day? Do I need to hire caregivers? Do I have enough money for that? What would happen to Laughing at My

Nightmare, Inc? Would I need to switch jobs? Could I support myself just writing? What if Hannah got burned out from my daily care? What if she decided she didn't like me and didn't want to live together? I'm quite annoying—it's not that unlikely. Would her parents see this as a negative thing? Would they allow it? What in the hell would my own parents have to say about it?

For so long, Hannah and I had dreamed about the day that we could say goodbye to our long-distance relationship and move in together. But now that the idea was being discussed as a serious, immediate option, I was forced to face the reality that so many people with SMA have faced before me: The transition from parental/family care to true independence is utterly overwhelming.

Overwhelming, but not impossible. And it was Hannah who helped me see that vital distinction. We began discussing the possibilities, in earnest, and as was always the case in our relationship, the more we put our minds to the challenges, the easier they seemed to be overcome.

A few days later, while driving home from a Laughing at My Nightmare event with Sarah, my phone buzzed with a text from Hannah. I'd been waiting for it all day. It read, "Took my mom out to dinner and broached the subject of you moving here. It went so well! She offered to help with anything we might need along the way."

My response did not quite capture the rush of happiness I was feeling. I replied, "Holyshitholyshitholyshit! Is this really happening?!"

Fast-forward a few months. It is March 20, 2018, and I am sitting in my van facing the house where I have spent the vast majority of my life. Surrounding my wheelchair are an impossible number of tightly crammed boxes, as well as lamps, a desk, a bath seat, a toilet chair, feeding tube supplies, breathing machines, and more. Hannah is in the driver's seat next to me. She's holding my hand. I'm smiling, half laughing, half sobbing uncontrollably. Andrew is standing on the front porch, waving goodbye. My mom and dad give me a hug and tell me they love me and that they are proud of me.

In the twenty-five years that I've been alive, I never fathomed that I'd be in this situation, leaving my parents' house to move halfway across the country with the girl I love, running

I'm so in love with her smile in this photo.

a successful nonprofit organization, writing books for a living, and feeling physically and mentally healthier than I've ever been. From the earliest days I can remember, my body, society, and the world around me have been feeding me the same message: You are sick and different and your existence is a pity. People are programmed to feel bad for me, knowing nothing about the quality of my life. At times, the outside perception that my life is negative and sad became so powerful that I internalized it and developed harmful beliefs that I was a burden to even the people who love me most.

It was largely my responsibility to shake off that idea and prove my worth, to show people that I am just as funny, intelligent, sexy, hardworking, adventurous, and successful as anyone else. My friends, family, and girlfriend played a crucial role in helping me achieve a healthy mind-set about society's misperceptions and my place within it. I owe them more than I can ever give them.

But as Hannah backs up the van and starts down the road, I am not thinking about society or my disability or being a burden. I'm thinking about driving up to our new apartment for the first time, and how amazing it's going to feel to fall asleep next to Hannah without a countdown of days together in the back of my mind. I'm thinking about how the hell we are going to shower me if the new bathtub is too small for my specialized seat. Maybe we can lay me in the sink? I'm thinking about writing more and reading more and traveling more. I'm thinking about whether it's too early to let out a small fart or if that's going to set a bad precedent for the next eighteen hours of driving.

I'm thinking about my brother and . . . nope, damnit, crying again. I'm thinking about the speaking engagement Sarah and I performed in North Carolina last week. Our company is still growing tremendously, and I'm thinking about the new programs we are working on to adjust to me living in Minnesota. Wow, Minnesota. Minnesota. I'm moving to Minnesota. I squeeze Hannah's hand a little tighter and she notices. Is that the Spinraza kicking in?

What happens from here is unknown. Life is strange and full of unexpected surprises, so I'm just going to close my eyes, enjoy the sunshine, and see where it takes me next.

Whoops, I let the fart out. Hannah is turning the van around and telling me it's over.

Acknowledgments

I want to thank both of the editors who contributed to the quality of this book—Claire, for helping me envision a true theme that would guide my essays, and Katherine, for shaping my attempts at chapters into beautiful finished products with your skillful touch. I want to thank my agent, Tina Dubois, for offering support and reassurance when I needed it most. Thank you to everyone at Roaring Brook Press for believing in me as a writer and a voice.

Thank you, Mom and Dad, for giving me the skills, values, responsibility, and confidence to be an independent adult. I love you both more than words could ever say.

Thank you to my brother, Andrew, for being there when shit gets rough, and for so much more that won't fit here. I'm insanely proud of the man you've become.

To Hannah, I love you forever. I'm not saying thank you, because you yell at me for that, but please know you are the best thing that's ever happened to me.